THE ELEMENTS OF SCRUM

by

Chris Sims

&

Hillary Louise Johnson

DYMAXICON

DYMAXICON

an imprint of
AGILE LEARNING LABS
502 Barbados Lane
Foster City, CA 94404
www.dymaxicon.com
First Edition

ISBN 978-0-9828669-1-7

The text of this book
is set in Calluna and Fontin,
both by Jos Buivenga.
The illustration font is
Complete in Him
by Kimberly Geswein.

FOR THE TEAM:
BETTY, STEVE & DAVID

VERSION 1.01
RELEASE NOTES

YOU'RE READING THE FIRST PUBLISHED VERSION of *The Elements of Scrum.* This is the annoying pop-up survey asking you for feedback as we prepare the next version. We want to know what about this book excites, inspires, scandalizes or perplexes you. Love that we included a section on retrospectives? Think the section on test-driven development is too skimpy—or that it doesn't belong in a book about scrum? Shocked that we don't capitalize the word "scrum"? Find a typesetting bug or dangling modifier? Have a burning, unanswered question? Then please head over to the Agile Learning Labs website and let us know what you think.

While you're there, you will also find a wealth of primary sources and other references cited in this book, as well as links to organizations and recommendations for further reading.

www.agilelearninglabs.com/the-elements-of-scrum

CONTENTS

A Week in the Life of a Scrum Team

IT'S 9:50 AM ON MONDAY, AND Brad is getting ready for his team's sprint planning meeting. Why does he seem so relaxed and happy, whistling while he works?

Brad is the product owner for a high-performing scrum team, and as usual, he will walk into the meeting with a good idea of what he would like the team to work on in the coming week-long sprint. Better yet, he will be greeted by people who are genuinely happy to see him and eager to find out what goodies he has brought. Once upon a time, meeting prep was a sweaty-palmed affair filled with Dilbertian angst, but Brad never thinks about those days anymore.

Brad's short list of work items, which includes both new features and bug-fixes, are the ones he deems the most important to complete on the project. He chooses them from a prioritized list called the product backlog, which is part of his domain as product owner.

As Brad selects features, he writes each one on an index card. The team refers to these work items as user stories, or simply stories—and yes, they do think of them as goodies. Coders delight in challenging, interesting work, and since they've had a hand in designing these user stories, they know the work will be stimulating.

Brad walks into the team's scrum room carrying his small stack of index cards. Frank, the team's scrum master, is already there making sure that the room is ready for the meeting. This is where the team does most of its work, and where they hold nearly all of their meetings. The walls are covered in hand-drawn charts and flip-chart pages with writing on them, including the team's agreed-upon definition of what it means to call a story "done."

One entire wall is devoted to the team's task board. This is a low-tech affair, composed of rows and columns marked off with blue painter's tape and populated by tasks written on sticky notes.

To the untrained eye the room looks as if a paper bomb just went off, but each and every scribble is a bit of meaningful information to the scrum team members, who like having their tasks, agreements, and progress charts in plain sight at all times. The company execs used to blanch visibly whenever they walked by this perfect storm of a workroom, but they've learned to trust the team's results; the CFO recently installed a task board for his own team, and has found that the billing department is finally getting invoices to vendors out on time.

Team members Mark and Jeff, the early-risers, are already present. Kira, Justus, Mick, Kai, and Malay filter in to the meeting by 10:00 AM.

Brad starts off: "The team has been getting an average of 40 story points' worth of work done each sprint. I have picked out eight stories, totaling 40 points' worth of work, right off the top of our product backlog. I'd like to see if the team will commit to these."

The stories are things that Brad, the business, and the customers want: stories have business value.

The team members discuss each story with Brad, making sure they understand what his acceptance criteria will be: the exact terms by which he will deem each story completed. They talk amongst themselves to understand how much and what type of work will need to be done to implement each of the requested stories.

During the discussion, the team members realize that one of the stories isn't as well-understood as they thought, and they ask Brad to go back to a key customer to get some more information. That story gets deferred, leaving the team with seven stories, for a total of 37 story points. Brad looks through the other items in the product backlog and selects three small stories worth one point each, and the team agrees that they can add these to the plan for this sprint.

There was a time when Brad would have tried to pressure the team into committing to more work, but he has learned that the team's velocity—the number of points it gets done each sprint—doesn't lie. Funnily enough, Brad saw the team's productivity actually go up once the company made a commitment to maintaining a sustainable pace and cut back on the crazy hours (although Malay still likes to burn the midnight oil if he is completely engrossed in a task).

In retrospect, Brad sees that the only thing he ever accomplished by pressuring them to take on "stretch goals" was to increase the bug count, thanks to the added stress and longer hours. Well, not the only thing—the pressure had also made him a bit of a bogeyman in the eyes of his fellows.

Now the development team trusts Brad, and its members view him as an equal and an ally. He in turn has learned that the team will let him know if they are going miss a commitment, or if they will be able to take on extra work, just as soon as they know it. He feels confident telling the customers that what's in the pipeline isn't a pipe dream.

It's 11:00 AM, and the team moves on to breaking the user stories down into tasks. In order for the team to implement each story, they need to break it down into the actual work tasks that need to be done. The team works together to figure out how each story will be designed, coded and tested. Along the way they record each task that will need to be done on a sticky note.

As noon approaches, the meeting is nearly over and the team has a plan for the coming week-long sprint. They call the plan their sprint backlog: it's a list of the stories that the team committed to, along with the tasks that will need to be done in order to complete the stories. They have also added a couple of team-improvement tasks to the sprint backlog: process improvement ideas they have come up with on their own. They write each task on a sticky note and slap them all into the "to do" column on their task board.

Before the meeting ends, the team uses a page of flip-chart paper to create a chart they will use to monitor their progress as they burn through their tasks over the coming week. They call this their sprint burn down chart.

Tuesday at 10:00 AM, the team gathers in a semi-circle in front of their task board for their daily scrum. The daily scrum is a short meeting that helps the team stay connected and coordinated. It is held standing up to encourage brevity, which is why they sometimes call this meeting the "daily stand-up."

Taking turns, each team member shares: which tasks they've completed in the previous day, which tasks they expect to complete before tomorrow's daily scrum, and anything that is getting in their way or slowing them down. Kira mentions that the code in the windowing library isn't behaving as she would expect. Kai offers to help her work it out right after the meeting. Mick says he's having trouble reproducing the bug he's working on, and Justus says that he can help with that. Mick and Justus make plans to team-up right after lunch.

The team members update their task board as they go, and everyone finds the ceremony of moving task stickies across the board extremely satisfying. In less than 15 minutes the meeting is over, and the team gets back to work, confident that they are on-track to meet their commitment to deliver the items in their sprint backlog.

At Wednesday's daily scrum, Brad reminds everyone to take a bit of time before that afternoon's "story time" meeting to review the short list of new and upcoming stories that he wants to work on in the meeting. When 3:00 PM rolls around, the team gets together to spend an hour refining the stories in their product backlog. Some teams call this "backlog grooming," but this team thinks that calling it "story time" is more fun.

"I've got six stories I'd like to review," says Brad. "Two are brand new, so we'll need to do story point estimation for them. The other four are big stories that I'd like us to break down into smaller stories; they are too big for the team to take into a sprint."

The team examines the four large stories first, finding

ways to break each one into several smaller stories, until the four big stories have become 15 small ones, each more detailed than the original.

Now they need to estimate how much work is represented by the 15 small stories and the two new stories that Brad introduced. Scrum master Frank leads the team through an "estimation game" he learned at a conference, which plays out almost like a card game and helps the team reach agreement quickly. By 3:45 PM, the team has assigned story point estimates to each of the stories, and Brad adjourns the meeting.

On his way back to his desk, Brad is thinking about where in the product backlog to put the stories that the team just groomed. He thinks at least two of them are high enough priority that he may put them at the top and try to get them scheduled into next week's sprint. He'll slot the rest into the product backlog according to their priority, some near the top, others farther down. Some will likely make it into the next product release, but some will be deferred until later.

At Thursday's daily scrum, the team identifies a new issue: one of the stories they committed to for the sprint is turning out to be more difficult than they previously thought; the story may not get done, they report.

Brad is upset to hear the news, but appreciates the early warning; he'll have the chance to manage the expectations of the team's stakeholders.

Mark and Malay decide to pair on the coding work for the at-risk story, and Mick offers to help automate the tests for it. Towards the end of the day, Kira finishes up another story and asks how she can help Mark, Malay, and Mick.

At Friday's daily scrum, the team still isn't sure that the at-risk story will be done in time for the big demo, but they are hopeful. Brad tells the team that he is available at a moment's notice to answer any questions the team has, or to sign-off on the story if they get it done. Right before lunch, Mark calls Brad over to show him the working software. Is it acceptable? Brad grins and tells the team, "I knew you could do it! Let's get some lunch. I'm buying."

Right after lunch, the team assembles for the public finale to their sprint, an event called the sprint review. The whole team is there, and they have invited all of the stakeholders to attend. Not every stakeholder comes every time, of course, but most find it valuable enough to attend frequently.

Anne, the VP of sales, has come to the meeting today. The team begins by announcing that they completed all of the stories that they had committed to for this sprint. Then they launch right into demonstrations of the software built for each story. Mick shows off a bug fix that will keep a key client happy. Justus shows the progress he has made in localization for the Japanese market. Finally, the team shows off the story that Anne was most keen to see—the very same one that almost didn't make it.

After the demo, the team invites the participants to try the new functionality for themselves, ask questions or make suggestions. Brad takes careful notes as the various stakeholders share their opinions of the current state of the product, and which changes they are hoping to see by release time. Brad thanks them all for their input and assures them that he will take it into consideration as he re-prioritizes the product backlog. The meeting wraps up and the stakeholders file out.

The team takes a short break before returning to their scrum room.

Now it's time for the very last part of the sprint, the team's retrospective. The whole scrum team is present: Brad, Frank, Kira, Mark, Jeff, Justus, Mick, Kai, and Malay. Nobody outside the scrum team is invited to the retrospective. The team talks openly about how the sprint went, and looks for areas in their process that could be improved.

Mark mentions that the pair programming he and Malay did together went very well; perhaps the team would be willing to pair more often? Kai would like to pair all the time, but others fear pairing might involve too much overhead, especially since the team has a working agreement to code-review all production code.

Jeff suggests that they modify their team agreement such that code could either be paired on, or reviewed. The team agrees. Mark, Kai, Malay, and Kira all agree to pair program at least one hour each day in the coming sprint. Jeff, Justus, and Mick each agree to try pair programming at least once in the next sprint. The team treats the pairing as an experiment, and they plan to review the results at the beginning of next Friday's retrospective.

Before calling it a day—and a sprint—the team members take a few minutes to recognize each other for all the things that led to the successful sprint. Brad is especially grateful to the team for delivering the at-risk story.

The team members head out to start their weekend feeling good and looking forward to doing it all over again next week.

PART I: INTRODUCTION TO AGILITY

I

In The Beginning: The Waterfall Method

IN 1901, A 63 YEAR-OLD DAREDEVIL named Annie Edson Taylor decided to go over Niagara Falls in a barrel for no obvious reason whatsoever. She survived with only a few bruises and gashes and declared, upon emerging, "I would sooner walk up to the mouth of a cannon, knowing it was going to blow me to pieces, than make another trip over the falls."

If you've ever worked on a big, messy enterprise-level software project that used the "waterfall" method, you probably know exactly how Annie felt. Surprisingly, however, the term waterfall does not owe itself to frustrated developers' identification with Annie's misadventure.

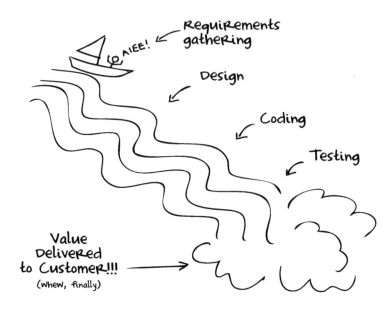

A "Traditional" Waterfall Process

Winston W. Royce first presented what is now known as the *traditional* waterfall method in a 1970 paper delivered at IEEE WestCom, an engineering conference. Royce didn't use the term waterfall, but he did describe a sequential process wherein each phase is completed before the next is begun. What you might not know is that Royce offered up this model as an example of how *not* to do software development!

Royce went on to say that of course one would never want to run a software project this way—and he next described an iterative process, much like today's agile methodologies, which he declared to be categorically superior. Still, somehow, the description of what would come to be known as waterfall clicked with his audience and became widely talked about.

The event that cemented waterfall's status as the trusted model for all enterprise-scale software development projects was the US Department of Defense's adoption, in 1985, of the waterfall method as the official standard for all projects carried out on the DOD's dime, whether by government agencies or independent defense contractors.

By the turn of the 21ˢᵗ Century, even the government had begun to get an inkling that the waterfall method might be flawed. An official 2005 NASA document describing the method noted that, "The standard waterfall model is associated with the failure or cancellation of a number of large systems. It can also be very expensive." The document went on to mention that something called "eXtreme Programming" looked quite promising.

Four years later, NASA gave a flurry of press interviews to announce that their engineers had devised their very own agile methodology called "Extreme Programming Maestro Style." We know, it sounds like something you would order with a side of fries at In-N-Out Burger, but NASA used it to write the software to control the Mars lander robot. Pretty cool, eh?

WATERFALL DEFINED

The waterfall method for developing and delivering enterprise software projects breaks the process into discrete stages like:

1. *requirements-gathering*
2. *design*
3. *coding*
4. *testing*

In a waterfall process, each step must be completed before moving on to the next, and all steps in the process must be completed before any value is delivered to the customer. You can see from the illustration on page 22 exactly where the name waterfall comes from—the development process literally flows from one stage to the next, moving the project inexorably downhill (often in every sense of the word).

Proponents of the waterfall method do, of course, have a rationale for the way they like to do things. For starters, waterfall lends itself to scheduling and reporting, allowing CEOS, CFOS, corporate attorneys and other stakeholders to use familiar tools and processes when it comes to writing contracts and allocating budgets. Make no mistake, getting these constituents to embrace change can be a lot more challenging than getting the most entrenched project managers and developers to come around to a more agile point of view.

On the design side, waterfall proponents cleave to a philosophy known as big design up front (BDUF), which is common to many plan-driven software development methodologies (The phrase and acronym are most often used by BDUF's detractors, spoken with a bit of a lip-curl, much the way some students use the phrase Big Man On Campus, or BMOC, to describe the "dumb jocks" at their school).

A common argument in favor of BDUF is that by "perfecting" the design before moving on to implementation, one can catch errors and bugs early, which reduces costs over the life of the project.

The fly in the ointment is that rather unrealistic word: *perfecting*. Now, if you are manufacturing an automobile, then a good case can indeed be made for getting your tooling right before moving into production. It is easy enough to ensure that your fenders will line up with your body panels when everything is still on paper, thus avoiding having to re-cast expensive dies and hold up the entire production process when you discover too late that they don't fit.

BDUF is predicated on the notion that it is possible to "perfect" a product's design before moving into production. And that may be true when it comes to car fenders... but software products are complex systems, not static objects, and systems designed in the absence of any real experiential data are famous for generating a muddle of unintended consequences—before they fail, leaving you with a big mess to clean up. "Communism is like Prohibition, it's a good idea but it won't work," Will Rogers famously said, and you could say much the same about BDUF.

In software development terms, this means that you can sit at the drawing board all day long, creating breathtakingly elegant theories that are a delight to behold—but the moment you begin putting it into practice, Whoa Nelly!—all kinds of unexpected consequences and complications begin to emerge. Worse yet, down the road your customer may just end up doing battle with the software equivalent of the Russian mafia.

2

Enter the Agilistas

Right now it's only a notion, but I think
I can get the money to make it into a
concept, and later turn it into an idea.
~ Woody Allen

IN 2001, SEVENTEEN SUPER-GEEKS GATHERED AT the Snowbird ski resort in Utah to explore a shared hunch about the future of software development. They included proponents of nascent methodologies like scrum, extreme programming, crystal, feature-driven development, and "others sympathetic to the need for an alternative to documentation driven, heavyweight software development processes," according to Jim Highsmith, who set down the events in writing for posterity. He fondly pointed out that "a bigger gathering of organizational anarchists would be hard to find."

Those assembled agreed upon a name for their movement: "agile." They dubbed themselves the Agile Alliance, and drafted an *Agile Manifesto*: a brief set of statements that would serve as the new movement's Declaration of Independence, Constitution and Bill of Rights all rolled into one. This napkin-sized document maps the common philosophical ground the Alliance members discovered over that weekend. What the members did not do was seek to codify any one set of practices or methods.

"The agile movement is not anti-methodology," Highsmith wrote, "in fact, many of us want to restore credibility to the word methodology. We want to restore a balance. We embrace modeling, but not in order to file some diagram in a dusty corporate repository."

None of this happened in a vacuum. The Agile Alliance was a reaction to the way software projects were commonly managed: development processes like waterfall that break planning, design, development and testing into a set of discrete steps, one after the other—down which development flowed freely and smoothly like water over Niagara... until crashing into the rocks at the bottom.

The times were ripe for change. In 1995 the Standish Group's annual "Chaos" report had detailed the shocking failure of traditional software development methods to deliver. According to the report, only 16% of traditionally-run enterprise software projects came in on time and on budget; 31% of projects would be cancelled, while 53% would run 189% over their original budgets. When surveyed as to why their projects failed so hard and so often, the number one cause IT managers cited was "lack of user involvement," with "incomplete requirements" a close second. That's right, even BDUF was not able to provide adequate requirements-gathering, despite the procedural emphasis placed on that phase of development.

Our founding Alliance members, despite their perhaps romantic penchant for referring to themselves as "anarchists," came from the ranks of those disgruntled IT managers who had seen and experienced the waterfall method's failings in action. They were experienced hands, not theorists, and they knew what worked, and what didn't.

Alistair Cockburn, a British IT strategist residing in Salt Lake City, had been working on a new methodology he called "crystal," based on his observation that the problem with rational, linear methodologies is that human beings are essentially non-linear—and all software development is done by humans. "We have been designing complex systems whose active components are variable and highly non-linear components called people, without characterizing these components or their effect on the system being designed," Cockburn told an audience of systems scientists and other technologists at a conference in 1999. "Upon reflection, this seems absurd, but remarkably few people in our field have devoted serious energy to understanding how these things called people affect software development."

At Chrysler Corporation, Kent Beck and Ron Jeffries had been collaborating with people like Ward Cunningham, the inventor of the wiki, on a developer-centric methodology known as "extreme programming," which included practices like test-driven development and pair programming.

And Jeff Sutherland, John Scumniotales, Jeff McKenna and Ken Schwaber had all been developing yet another iterative methodology they called "scrum."

These and other early agile theorists were all present at Snowbird, and they had all come to believe independently that iterative methodologies were the future.

THE ITERATIVE METHOD

One key problem with BDUF is that it assumes perfect knowledge of the future. But anyone who has worked on an enterprise-scale software project knows that the only thing you can count on is change. Agile processes of all kinds share one thing: they embrace change, approaching it as an opportunity for growth, rather than an obstacle.

Agile teams do the same development work that waterfall teams do, but they do it very differently. The agile development cycle employs the same functions as the waterfall method: requirements-gathering, design, coding and testing.

The simple view into how agile development differs from waterfall development is this: an agile team, instead of completing each step *before* moving on to the next one never to return, does a *little bit* of requirements gathering, a *little bit* of design, coding and testing, and delivers a *little bit* of value to the customer. Then the team does it all over again... and again, refining and tweaking processes as work progresses, until the project is complete.

But incremental, iterative development changes not just when you do things, but how you do them. Agile iterations (called "sprints" in scrum) are not miniature waterfalls; in agile processes, there really are no steps. Agile development is a holistic process, meaning that testing, design, coding and requirements gathering are fully integrated, interdependent processes. Testing, for example, is folded into the design process. Requirements aren't simply gathered; instead, a deep, shared understanding of them is cultivated through constant communication between the team, the product owner and the customer.

But what does this look like in practice? How do you *do*

agile development? Whether you adopt scrum, lean, extreme programming, or create your own melange of several agile methodologies, you will:

Test as you go, not at the end—a bug fixed now is cheaper than one that has had a chance to propagate through a system for months.

Deliver product early and often, as only by demonstrating working software to your customer can you find out what they *really* want. Because agile processes include constant feedback from customers, projects stay relevant and on track, and because each increment is complete upon delivery, agile development serves to mitigate risk: should a project be cancelled, then the customer may still use the software delivered to date.

Document as you go, and only as needed. When you bake the documentation into your process, you only write documentation that is relevant and useful.

Build cross-functional teams to break down silos, so that no individual or department can become a process or information bottleneck.

The main idea behind the agile approach is to deliver business value immediately, in the form of working software, and to continue delivering value in regular increments. As we'll see in the next chapter, the benefits a business can realize from doing development work iteratively are both immediate and cumulative.

3

AGILE VALUES & PRINCIPLES

It is important that an aim never be defined in terms of activity or methods. It must always relate directly to how life is better for everyone.
~ *W. Edwards Deming*

My aim is not to teach the method that everyone ought to follow in order to conduct his reason well, but solely to reveal how I have tried to conduct my own.
~ *René Descartes*

DO NOT LET THE IDEALISTIC TONE of the *Agile Manifesto* fool you into thinking that it was composed by a bunch of starry-eyed dreamers or ivory tower dwellers; the authors were all battle-scarred veterans of the wild and woolly days of early software development, and they based their tenets on what they had learned in the field. Because of this, the values and principles devised by the founders of the Agile Alliance stand up well; every day we seen how applicable they are to real-world software projects.

Below is our annotated discussion of each of the values and principles that together comprise the *Agile Manifesto*.

THE AGILE VALUES

> *Individuals and interactions over processes and tools*
> *Working software over comprehensive documentation*
> *Customer collaboration over contract negotiation*
> *Responding to change over following a plan*

Like most true things, the agile values sound simple and obvious when you first hear them, and they remain unchanged from the day the Agile Alliance founders first published them as part one of the *Agile Manifesto*.

But putting these values into daily practice—and cleaving to them day in and day out through thick and thin—demands a Zen-like rigor. If you have been part of a command-and-control work (or school) environment for any length of time, you will have to practice these values consciously until you have fully absorbed them and they become second nature to you—and this is true even if the dulcet tones of the agile values thrill you to your very soul. Old habits die hard, whether they are habits we formed willingly or otherwise.

And if you've been in a command-and-control environment long enough to be commanding and controlling others, you may be sputtering something like "Hold your horses! Wait one gosh darned minute there... how can we serve real clients without tools, documentation, contracts or plans?!?"

The answer is: You cannot. Nor does agility demand that you do.

Notice how each value is stated so that it favors one factor "over" another—and not "instead of" another? The agile philosophy is not about "musts," "shoulds," absolutes or trade-offs. This is what makes agile thinking so powerful and flexible, as well as so subtle and slippery! There is no rule book to follow or refer to, only values and principles to internalize.

Let's take a look at each of the agile values in a bit more depth:

Individuals and interactions over processes and tools

One of the basic tenets of agility is that the people who do the work know best how to get that work done. Let's say that all six of your teams prefer to create estimates by playing *Planning Poker*. Now, when you spin up a new team, do you instruct them that they must use *Planning Poker*? If you are practicing an agile development methodology like scrum or extreme programming, the answer is an emphatic no! You want each self-organizing team of individuals to use the tools that work best for them. Might you suggest that the new team try *Planning Poker* for a sprint or two, since it works so well for the other teams? Absolutely! It is good practice to arrive at decisions like which tools to use through trial and error—the process of inspecting and adapting.

But think about this: you and the rest of your teams will never know if there is a better tool out there than *Planning Poker* if you forbid or discourage experimentation.

There are agile tools, methodologies and processes out there in abundance, and you should endeavor to sample them all—tools and processes are splendid, useful things, so long as they remain where they belong, in the hands of the human beings who use them. Processes and tools need to serve people, not vice versa.

Working software over comprehensive documentation

This is another subtle doozy that invites misinterpretation. Documentation is fine when it serves the purpose of creating value and moving a project forward in an expedient manner. For example, user documentation is a valuable part of most products. Problems arise when the focus moves away from the product itself, and on to things like process documentation: "Remember to use the new cover sheets on your TPS reports!"*

When you begin your development process by investing heavily in comprehensive up-front documentation (remember BDUF from our discussion of the waterfall method?), you sacrifice the opportunity to inspect and adapt, learning from your mistakes and adjusting your process and your requirements as you go. It's only human nature to become attached to something you worked hard to produce; if you spend the same amount of time drafting your documentation as Tolstoy spent writing *War and Peace*, you may find yourself treating your masterpiece as if it were the work product itself.

A common misapprehension is that agile teams don't document or plan; but in practice, agile teams actually spend more time and energy on planning and documentation than traditional teams, because the plan is always being elaborated upon and updated. On an agile software project, the plan is all around you, in the form of user stories, backlogs,

---

*If you haven't seen the movie *Office Space,* go rent it now, otherwise you won't get this joke.

acceptance tests, and big, visible charts; these are all part of your communication-rich environment. An agile plan is a living thing that accrues and evolves over the life of a project; it is never a weighty tome to be deferred to as scripture. This means that at any given point in time, the plan represents our current best understanding of the project, but we expect it to evolve and improve as we inspect and adapt.

So, where does your agile team turn for answers, if not the documentation? You turn to the working software: everything you have built, tested and integrated to date. If you have working software, automated tests, an up-to-date product backlog, and an actively participating product owner, you have everything you need to move forward as efficiently and effectively as possible.

Customer collaboration over contract negotiation

This agile value also seeks to abolish the spectre of up-front planning, but with a special emphasis on keeping the dialogue between the development team and the customer as open and fluid as possible. We all know that contracts are good and necessary things, especially when they honor and protect all parties, as well-drafted contracts do.

Many of the founders of the Agile Alliance were consultants, so they were familiar with the pitfalls of contract work, where the contractor's bid is often no more than a bet that they can get the work done in a certain amount of time, with their profit dependent upon how quickly and cheaply they can meet the customer's minimum requirements. If you've ever had your kitchen remodeled, you know the kind of mildly adversarial relationship a bid-based contract entails. Sure, the contract protects you against overcharges, but not against cut corners and minimal execution, especially once your poor, honest contractor realizes you're a meddlesome, fussy pain in the neck and that he bid too low and is going to lose his shirt. Bottom line: are you really getting the best kitchen, for the best price, that you possibly could? Unless the contractor is your brother-in-law, probably not.

The *Agile Manifesto's* authors ultimately concluded that contract-based projects emphasize the wrong things. They preferred a time-and-materials model where all parties work together as partners to build the most valuable system they can within the specified time and budget. The customer's risk is mitigated not by an up-front guarantee that puts the contractor at risk, but by their constant involvement in the process and by an agile team's ability to deliver increments of working software on a regular basis.

The efficiencies created by following an agile framework, in which working software is delivered early and often, also guarantee that the customer will realize the maximum value for the time and money invested, further obviating the need for up-front contract negotiation.

Responding to change over following a plan

Plan-driven organizations usually have in place "change control" processes designed with the best of intentions: to prevent your project from suffering mission creep, feature creep, and other nefarious forms of attrition and bloat. A worthy goal! But there is a rub. Change control can only work in a context in which change is actually controllable. If you're running a lab that is conducting tests on pharmaceuticals, you'll need a high degree of control, in order to ensure your test results are consistent. Uncontrolled change on this kind of project could render your work worthless.

Software development, however, bears little resemblance

to double-blind drug testing. It is a process fraught with unknowns, a journey of discovery.

Here is another metaphor: If you were setting out to sail across the English Channel, you would be foolish to embark with nothing but a chart and a hardened plan. To succeed in reaching Dover, you would need to leave Callais carrying a compass, and you would need to use it frequently, correcting your course constantly as you fought against the vagaries of wind and current.

In software development, change is as inevitable as weather at sea, so it stands to reason that the best process is one in which change is also good. Planning on a software project must be fluid, not fixed, for the good of the team, but mainly for the good of the product, and ultimately for the good of the customer. This is why you plan for change and change your plan—pretend that you can succeed by doing otherwise and you will eventually find yourself adrift in the middle of nowhere.

Agilists love to point out that while traditional methods of software development are plan-driven, agile projects are *planning* driven. Being agile is about building a flexible process that anticipates and embraces change, allowing the team to adapt to new requirements and unexpected developments. It is a by-now-familiar refrain: inspect and adapt. Notice how that mantra surfaces in every discussion of every agile value?

If you're finding all of these values a bit much to sort out, just grab a sharpie and a sheet of paper and write "Inspect & Adapt" on it in capital letters. Now tape the piece of paper to the wall with blue painter's tape, up high where everyone on your team can see. Refer to as needed. When you stop needing to refer to the piece of paper, come back to the values. You should find that they all make perfect sense now—and you got there the agile way, by choosing a manageable increment of work to accomplish, and inspecting and adapting!

AGILE PRINCIPLES

The agile principles can be seen as a further elaboration on, and practical application of, the agile values; they are the other half of the *Agile Manifesto*. We recommend printing these out and posting them on the wall, embroidering them on a throw pillow, or spray-painting them on a freeway over-pass.... Just kidding. Tattooing them on your forearm will do nicely:

1. *Our highest priority is to satisfy the customer through early and continuous delivery of valuable software.*

2. *Welcome changing requirements, even late in development. Agile processes harness change for the customer's competitive advantage.*

3. *Deliver working software frequently, from a couple of weeks to a couple of months, with a preference to the shorter timescale.*

4. *Business people and developers must work together daily throughout the project.*

5. *Build projects around motivated individuals. Give them the environment and support they need, and trust them to get the job done.*

6. *The most efficient and effective method of conveying information to and within a development team is face-to-face conversation.*

7. *Working software is the primary measure of progress.*

8. *Agile processes promote sustainable development. The sponsors, developers, and users should be able to maintain a constant pace indefinitely.*

9. *Continuous attention to technical excellence and good design enhances agility.*

10. *Simplicity—the art of maximizing the amount of work not done—is essential.*

11. *The best architectures, requirements, and designs emerge from self-organizing teams.*

12. *At regular intervals, the team reflects on how to become more effective, then tunes and adjusts its behavior accordingly.*

Now let's look at each principle in a bit more detail:

1. *Our highest priority is to satisfy the customer through early and continuous delivery of valuable software.*

If, as the Standish Group's "Chaos" report claims, 20-30% of projects fail, and the majority run significantly over budget, then what was the "highest priority" on those projects? Not the stated priority, but the real priority? Let's give those teams credit and assume that their highest priority wasn't something so crass as "running out the clock while looking busy" or "covering our backsides by fulfilling the letter of the contract even as we run out of runway without delivering anything." No, let us assume that their priority was something more noble, like "Following our plan to the letter however obsolete it becomes," or "Working around the clock to meet the unrealistic deadline set by our stakeholders."

Have you ever worked on a project where the *de facto* priority was satisfying a cranky manager instead of the customer? Priority = office politics. Where you had to stay late to get any real work done because you had so many mandatory meetings? Priority = bureaucracy. Where you knew the feature you were building would never ship, but kept your head down and built it anyway? Priority = organizational conformity.

Putting the customer first and promising to deliver value continuously introduces checks and balances into the delivery pipeline, and these prevent people and organizations from slip-sliding into behaviors that serve the organization instead of the customer. Organizations that adopt agile methods usually experience significant growing pains as these types of misguided priorities are rooted out and exposed to the air.

> 2. *Welcome changing requirements, even late in development. Agile processes harness change for the customer's competitive advantage.*

One of our favorite technology stories ever involves a startup called Confinity, which had an obscure software product you may never have heard of: PayPal. In the early days, Confinity's core product was a method of "beaming" money between Palm Pilots. The founders doubtless imagined individuals would use this technology to do such momentous tasks as lending each other twenty bucks and splitting restaurant checks. As a secondary feature, they added the ability to send payments via e-mail. Well, this second-string idea became the killer app, and the founders possessed the agility to recognize where their competitive advantage lay. They were able to change their product's requirements radically to take advantage of a huge opportunity.

Stuff happens: Technologies shift suddenly. Competitors bring surprises to the market. Regulatory landscapes change. Recessions hit industries. Geniuses make discoveries in the middle of the night. Your team shouldn't need to call in FEMA to incorporate minor or even major changes to your requirements.

3. *Deliver working software frequently, from a couple of weeks to a couple of months, with a preference to the shorter timescale.*

Hillary once attended an event called Startup Weekend, where a couple hundred aspiring tech entrepreneurs gathered together on a Friday evening to pitch ideas, then formed small teams and worked feverishly over a 52 hour period, launching actual online start-up companies on Sunday evening.

This is an extreme example of the axiom: the less time you have, the more efficiently you must work. The teams at Startup Weekend did not have time for extensive planning meetings. Most teams began coding within an hour of forming, starting with the most essential features of a website and designing their product as they went. All 28 of the startups that formed that weekend presented working demos on Sunday evening, and quite a few had launched fully functioning web apps.

Okay, so that is not the method by which you'd want to build a scheduling system for an airline, or a financial services database app, but what enterprise teams can glean from this example is the lesson that short cycles lead to improved efficiency of effort.

Many teams think the best way to ease into being agile is to start with a long sprint cycle, but the opposite is generally true. A short cycle forces you to focus on the essential and do away with productivity-sapping habits from your waterfall days. Nothing cuts down on meeting bloat more than knowing you have to deliver working software every seven days!

> 4. *Business people and developers must work together daily throughout the project.*

Both sides have been known to resist this one. Business people waltz in asking ill-informed questions and making silly demands, say the developers. And for their part, business people may see developers as arrogant, eccentric types who care more about the abstract beauty of their code than they do about the end product.

Well, if the two factions only see each other once a month, then guess what? Those judgments will be true! Regular collaboration allows the business people to appreciate the technical challenges and opportunities that the developers face. Regular collaboration also helps the technical people understand and share the vision held by the business' stakeholders. Collaboration between business people and developers should be like voting in Chicago: do it early and do it often!

> 5. *Build projects around motivated individuals. Give them the environment and support they need, and trust them to get the job done.*

Software development is not an industrial process, and software development team members are not interchangeable warm bodies performing rote tasks on an assembly line. Yet a common complaint among developers is that the businesses they work for can seem to treat them like faceless "human resources." Little wonder developers ruefully describe themselves as "code monkeys."

The good news is that almost all software development teams are comprised of highly skilled, sometimes troublesome, and uniquely valuable human beings. These are experts with a capacity to feel passionate about their work. Give them the space and freedom they need, and expect great results in return.

> 6. *The most efficient and effective method of conveying information to and within a development team is face-to-face conversation.*

Have you ever worked at a cube farm? You know, a place where everyone sits in a cubicle and communicates with one another by text and e-mail, even though they're all in the same room? Agile teams are far more likely to work in an open, shared space, and to communicate verbally whenever possible. Why? Because agility is a communication-rich affair.

A study by two academic psychologists at New York University and University of Chicago demonstrated that people reading e-mail correctly interpreted the sender's intended tone only 56% of the time—yet they believed they had correctly interpreted it 90% of the time. Telephone conversationalists fared much better. But face-to-face communication, where nuances of expression and gesture enhance meaning, is the best of all.

This principle is sometimes misinterpreted by proponents of agile methods as meaning that distributed teams cannot be agile. But notice that the principle only states that face-to-face is best. You can practice agile teamwork remotely, but you might want to take special care in how you set up your communication streams.

At our company, Agile Learning Labs, we have one team

member who joins us remotely via video conference for our daily scrum. Once a week or so, we try to have an in-person day, and we do monthly retrospectives in person as well. If your team is too far-flung—India and Wyoming, say—see if you can find budget to fly everybody in for a project kick-off. Arguably, the most valuable part of face-to-face communication occurs during the getting-to-know-you phase. Once your team has bonded, remote communication can flow quite well in our experience.

> 7. *Working software is the primary measure of progress.*

This principle is simple enough: the proof is in the pudding. Not the grocery list. Not the recipe. Not the grandeur of the chef's kitchen. Not the silver spoon that serves it up. Just the pudding.

You may notice that this principle relates directly to principle number one ("Our highest priority is to satisfy the customer through early and continuous delivery of valuable software."). If your priorities are correctly aligned, then you will produce working software.

> 8. *Agile processes promote sustainable development. The sponsors, developers, and users should be able to maintain a constant pace indefinitely.*

We've all experienced "crunch time"—that end phase of a project when we all stay late and seemingly live, sleep and eat the work in a state of amplified productivity; but software shops have been known to carry this practice to the extreme. In 2004, the spouse of a developer at game publisher Electronic Arts caused a major controversy when she published a rant about the company's mandatory 85 hour work week for all developers—a "crunch time" schedule that was permanent. The kerfuffle ultimately resulted in EA settling a lawsuit for millions with their designers and programmers, and software shops everywhere began reconsidering the wisdom of the custom of long hours for developers. What you may not know (and EA certainly didn't), is that extreme work hours actually lower productivity overall, rather than raising it.

Why the software industry took this wholesale detour into crazy working hours is a bit mystifying to us, particularly as we have plenty of historical evidence that overworking people yields poor results in any field. Henry Ford knew this, and scandalized the industrial world when he introduced the five day week and eight hour day in 1926—down from six days and ten hours. Ford told the magazine *World's Work*, "A full week's wage for a short week's work will pay." He was right— net productivity went up on the shorter schedule, not down. And while knowledge work differs from manufacturing work in many ways, it remains true that humans have only so much effort to expend before cognitive function declines enough that we begin to make mistakes, and in software development, that means more bugs.

9. *Continuous attention to technical excellence and good design enhances agility.*

Agility is not about cutting corners to go faster. Anyone who has worked in a cluttered up, ill-maintained legacy code base will attest to the fact that progress comes slowly when those who went before us took shortcuts.

By contrast, when the team pays ongoing attention to the design, architecture, testing, and cleanliness of their code, it is much easier to make changes. This increases the teams ability to deliver value quickly.

Some believe that because agile teams don't do big design up front, that they skimp on design and architecture. Not so! An agile team does this work all the time. When the team makes a change, they inspect and adapt their architecture, design, technical documentation, test code coverage, etc. Over the course of the project an agile team does more of these activities than most traditional teams do, but they do them just in time. In this way, the architecture is always appropriate for the current state of the code, not too much, not too little.

Agile team members are always improving their technical skills because they learn from each other. The time invested learning about test-driven development, design patterns, and new state-of-the-art practices pays rewards over the life of the project.

> *10. Simplicity—the art of maximizing the amount of work not done—is essential.*

The Standish Group's 2002 "Chaos" study of software project success and failure rates states that in a typical software system, 45% of features are never used. Only 7% of features are always used, and another 13% are used often.

When you do big design up front, you have only one chance, at the beginning of the project, to spec out everything you might possibly want in the product, from the necessary—a menu, a login page, a database—to the wildest of unnecessary and ill-advised follies—a pop-up survey, or... Hey! How about an animated paper clip?

On an agile project, you build the important bits first, and the ones you never get to are the ones you needed the least. Features that reveal themselves to be superfluous or just plain silly can fall off the backlog naturally, even as unplanned-for necessities—an Android app, an extra layer of security—are added on the fly.

    II. *The best architectures, requirements, and designs emerge from self-organizing teams.*

The common argument in favor of leaving architecture to the architects is that it takes an expert with a vision to craft a thing of elegance. As the joke goes: "What do you call a camel?" To which the snappy comeback is: "A horse designed by a committee." But there are two flaws in that reasoning.

First: there is a world of difference between a team and a committee. A team is a group of skilled individuals functioning in sync to achieve a common goal. A committee... well, a committee is a group of people who have nothing better to do than to sit on a committee. The Chicago Bulls are a team. Ocean's 11 are a team. The MPAA Ratings Board is a committee.

The second false assumption is that a software project is a thing. The goal of a software project is never to make a thing, but to build a system that solves a problem. And problem-solving is a task at which teams far outpace even very talented individuals. You may well have a brilliant architect on your agile team, but on a scrum team, she is not "The Architect." The team will value her expertise as an important resource and often look to her for guidance. The architecture will have her fingerprints all over it, but she won't be "in charge of the architecture." The team shares that responsibility equally. In practice, this means that what they are responsible for is cooperating with one another and putting the project itself first. Self-organizing teams don't leave behind individual contributions; the only thing they leave behind are egos.

> *12. At regular intervals, the team reflects on how to be-*
> *come more effective, then tunes and adjusts its be-*
> *havior accordingly.*

Individuals, teams and organizations have one trait in common: they are all susceptible to lapsing into bad habits and falling into ruts. To do so is human, and if it's any consolation, we fall into good habits all the time, too. A major part of any agile process—some might say the most important part—is inspecting and adapting at regular intervals, amplifying what works and revamping what doesn't work.

A powerful tool for accomplishing this fine-tuning is the retrospective, an activity focused on learning from what has just occurred and directly applying that learning to make things better going forward. Retrospectives are useful between iterations, between releases, and after any unusual incidents.

The agile retrospective is far more powerful than it appears at first glance. Some teams that are new to agile processes think they might save time by skipping the retrospective. Don't! In fact, we'd venture to say that if you were to take just *one* step toward agility, you should make it the inclusion of the retrospective in your work flow. Nothing will prove the value of iterative development more quickly than realizing the huge benefits to be had by regularly inspecting and improving the way you work. Retrospectives are covered in detail in chapter seven.

4

The Business Case for Agility

Chains of habit are too light to be felt
until they are too heavy to be broken.
~ Warren Buffet

"DELIVER EARLY, DELIVER OFTEN." IT IS an oft-repeated motto amongst all stripes of agilistas, scrum enthusiasts included. But deliver what, you say? Prototypes? Plans? Versions? Status reports? Pizza pies?

An agile team's deliverable may go by many different names, including "working software," "potentially shippable product," or our favorite: "business value."

So, without further ado, let's get down to brass tacks, as the business people like to say, and demonstrate in concrete terms just how an agile approach to software development delivers business value. We will do so by walking you through a typical software project, tracking revenue and spending for both an agile model and a waterfall model. Let the agile vs waterfall smackdown begin!

THE AGILE VS WATERFALL BUSINESS VALUE SMACKDOWN

Here is the breakdown of our fictional team and their resources for our example project:

> *6 engineers*
> *1 product manager (½ time)*
> *1 project manager (½ time)*
> *budget: $1M/year*
> *development time: 1.5 years*
> *expected revenue: $6M/year*

Let us compare the financials of this two-year project quarter-by-quarter, agile vs waterfall. Happy bean counting!

SMACKDOWN: ROUND ONE

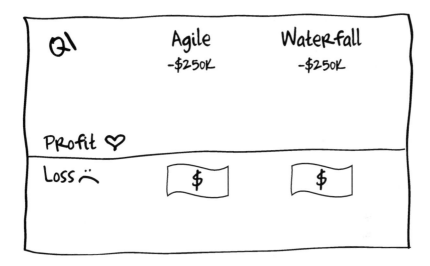

Q1: *Our teams are up and running! The agile team delivered their first small release at the end of the first quarter of development. The waterfall team is busy gathering requirements. No revenue has come in for either project, so the company is out $250,000 at this point either way.*

SMACKDOWN: ROUND TWO

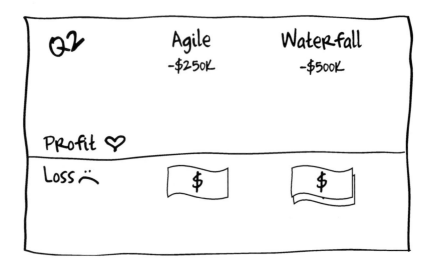

Q2: *The small bit of functionality that the agile team delivered at the end of last quarter has managed to generate some income. $250K isn't much, but it's enough that the project is now self-funding. What's more, the agile team has just delivered another increment of functionality.*

Meanwhile, the company executing this project using the waterfall approach has had to put another $250,000 into the project. They have some very nice requirements documents now....

SMACKDOWN: ROUND THREE

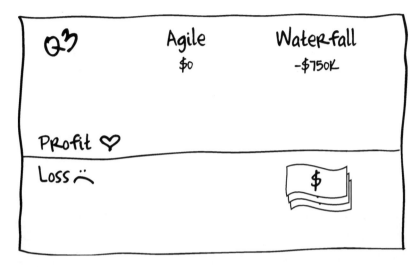

Q3: *The agile project generated a bit more revenue, and has now reached the break-even point. The waterfall team is doing design and architecture work, and has some really neat UML diagrams now! Management is starting to wonder if those diagrams are really worth the $750,000 that they have invested in this project so far.*

SMACKDOWN: ROUND FOUR

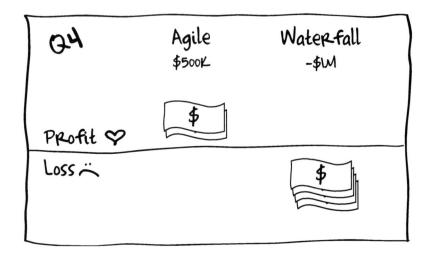

Q4: *The agile team has by now delivered even more, resulting in $1.5M total revenue by the end of Q4, which more than offsets the $1M in costs for the project so far. Note that $1.5M is equal to the entire project's budget—in other words, the agile team has already paid for the whole project. It's all profit from here on out!*

Over in waterfall land? Well, coding is taking a bit longer than expected. Not to worry! They will simply cut the testing time down. Management is getting really grumpy about the million dollars they have spent. There is some talk of scrapping the project altogether....

SMACKDOWN: ROUND FIVE

Q5: *Things are humming along nicely in agile-land! The project is almost fully implemented, and the team has had the chance to adjust some of the functionality based on customer feedback. Management is pretty happy, as they know they could stop the project now and continue to reap the income of the existing system. The project has already made the company $1.25M.*

Things are looking up for the waterfall project. They've made it into the testing phase, and it is actually going fairly well. Sure, they'll have to pull some functionality out here and there, as it would be too risky to fix it this late in the game, but that's expected. Right? At least they have stayed on-budget, and the company is only out the expected $1.25M so far. Wait a minute... Isn't that how much money the agile project has already made in profit?

SMACKDOWN: ROUND SIX

Q6: *Both teams deliver their software on time (this is, after all, just a simulation), and the waterfall project will finally start generating revenue. Did you see the new sports cars that the agile folks just bought?*

SMACKDOWN: ROUND SEVEN

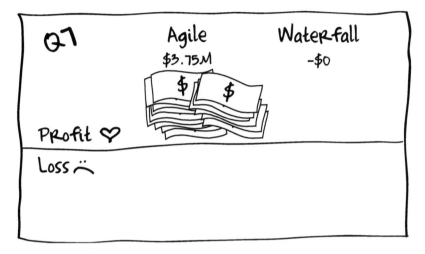

Q7: *Management at the waterfall shop is finally relaxing. The software has earned enough to pay back the cost of developing it. Meanwhile, management over at the agile company just announced a dividend for their shareholders, and bonuses for all employees.*

SMACKDOWN: FINAL ROUND

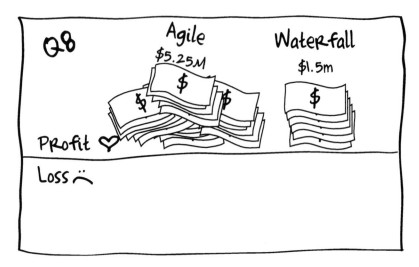

Q8: *Six months after development has ended, the agile project has generated more than double the profit of the waterfall project, despite the fact that they are earning revenue at exactly the same rate. The project's ROI, and the initial investment needed to complete it, are exponentially affected by the choice of development process, as can be seen in the performance table below:*

2 YEAR PERFORMANCE

Agile	Waterfall
Break Even: Q3	Break Even: Q7
Investment: $250K	Investment: $1.5M
Profit: $5.25M	Profit: $1.5M
ROI: 2,100%	ROI: 100%

We've barely scratched the surface of agile development as a tool for the creation of business value, and its salutary effect on ROI. *For an in-depth treatment of the financial impact of incremental development, the go-to book is* Software By Numbers: Low-Risk, High-Return Development *by Mark Denne and Jane Cleland-Huang. There you'll find these same ideas illustrated with plenty of examples drawn from real software projects and enough hard data to satisfy even the wonkiest of* CFOs.

PART II: SCRUM

5

A Brief History of Scrum

"Scrum: A team-based framework to develop complex systems and products."
~ *The Scrum Alliance*

"Scrum, as defined, actually doesn't say anything about software. Scrum is about work management and team dynamics that can be used in non-software projects."
~ *Jeff McKenna*

THE FIRST SCRUM TEAM WAS FORMED in 1993, when Jeff Sutherland, then VP of Object Technology at Easel Corporation, was inspired to take a new approach to a critical software project. The team who helped develop the new methodology included Jeff McKenna, then an object-oriented consultant, and John

Scumniotales, for whom Easel was a first development job out of college. All three would go on to be founding signatories of the *Agile Manifesto*.

Sutherland was jazzed by ideas he had encountered in a book called *Wicked Problems, Righteous Solutions: A Catalog of Modern Engineering Paradigms*, by Peter DeGrace and Leslie Hulet Stahl. DeGrace and Hulet Stahl were themselves influenced by a famous 1986 Harvard Business Review article by Hirotaka Takeuchi and Ikujiro Nonaka, "The New New Product Development Game," which first used the rugby "scrum" as a metaphor for a new kind of teamwork. The article described a product development team that would take "a holistic or 'rugby' approach—where a team tries to go the distance as a unit, passing the ball back and forth." DeGrace and Hulet Stahl took the ideas that worked in Japanese product design and manufacturing and began looking for analogous cases in software development, describing several "all-at-once" systems that they proposed were superior to linear waterfall processes.

Sutherland described his model for a better way as being based on what takes place in the head of an ace developer: "The simplest all-at-once model is a single super-programmer creating and delivering an application from beginning to end. All aspects of the development process reside in one person's head." The obvious benefits were "good internal architectural consistency," and the drawbacks were the lack of scalability and difficulty of knowledge transfer—who maintains the system once the super-programmer has left the building?

Sutherland and company set about designing a software development model that would let a close-knit team function as one, hoping to create a team with the powers of a multi-headed super-programmer! They called it scrum. Sutherland gives a detailed account of what followed, starting with the pitch meeting:

> *The CEO agreed that no plan ever delivered the required functionality on time. Many delays had been extensive and hurt the company financially.... He had never seen a promised delivery date met, and worse, he rarely discovered slippage until it was too late to reforecast company revenue.*
>
> *I told the CEO that in adopting scrum, we set the objectives at the beginning of what scrum refers to as a sprint. It is the team's responsibility to determine how to best meet those objectives. During the sprint, no one can bother team members with requests. At the end of a sprint, I added, working code will be demonstrated, so you can see the progress made. You can decide to ship anytime or do another sprint to get more functionality. Visible working code provides more confidence than extensive documentation with no operational system.*

The CEO went for it, and six months later, the team delivered the product on time, with the confidence to offer customers a guarantee. They did it with daily scrums, regular sprint reviews, and a smattering of practices from extreme programming. Remarkably, the process Sutherland describes in great detail is virtually unchanged from what you are reading about in the rest of this book.

Meanwhile, Ken Schwaber, then CEO of Advanced Development Methods, Inc., was experiencing "breakthrough productivity" by using some of the same ideas from

Japanese manufacturing. Schwaber suspected that the secret to the success of this new method lay in his use of empirical processes (inspect and adapt), rather than defined processes (plan and execute), but he wanted a second opinion, so he asked scientists at DuPont's Advanced Research Facility to give him a critical assessment of the industry standard for managing enterprise software projects with a (defined) waterfall process.

The DuPont scientists were aghast at what they deemed little more than pseudo-science: "We are most amazed that your industry treats these ill-formed processes as defined, and performs them without controls despite their irregular nature. If chemical processes that we don't understand completely were handled in the same way, we would get very unpredictable results."

Schwaber felt vindicated: a software project is too complex and chaotic to be managed via defined processes. The genius and agility of Sutherland's super-programmer can't be replicated through all the up-front planning in the world.

Sutherland and Schwaber were past collaborators and well aware of one another's work; scrum was born when they collaborated on a 1995 paper for a conference called Object-Oriented Programming, Systems, Languages & Applications (OOPSLA) that formalized and made public the scrum framework.

Physicist Mike Beedle first heard about scrum concepts from Sutherland. "His main idea about scrum was to create a team that would resemble artificial life, a robot, or an adaptive system, that would adapt and learn through 'social intelligence,'" Beedle wrote in 2010. Beedle combined early scrum practices with organizational pattern concepts he gleaned from the writings of computer scientist Jim Coplien, to dramatically rescue a multi-million dollar software project. "Eighty consultants; hundreds of employees; thousands of pages of documentation that included processes, procedures, requirements, design, testing; and hundreds of failed project plans, could not deliver what scrum and Org Patterns delivered in 4 months with 10 people. It was amazing."

Beedle and Schwaber were both present for the drafting of the *Agile Manifesto*, and the two collaborated on the book *Agile Software Development with Scrum,* which appeared in October of the same year. The following year, Schwaber co-founded the Scrum Alliance with Esther Derby and Mike Cohn. Schwaber also designed a curriculum for certifying individuals in scrum, and the designation Certified Scrum-Master (CSM) was born, followed by Certified Scrum Product Owner (CSPO), Certified Scrum Practitioner (CSP), Certified Scrum Trainer (CST) and Certified Scrum Coach (CSC). As of this writing, the Scrum Alliance has certified over 100,000 people.

Schwaber and the Scrum Alliance eventually parted ways (as founders and their companies so often do), but by then scrum was firmly established as the most widely-adopted and well-known agile methodology in current practice. Human resource departments everywhere now commonly approve requests for scrum certification for development and project management staff, and many are making scrum certification a prerequisite for hiring. If people today sometimes ask "Which should I choose—agile or scrum?" that's because scrum, although merely one of many agile methodologies, may well be the better-known of the two terms. (The answer to that question, by the way, is simply a resounding "Yes!")

While Schwaber focused on building an institution, Sutherland stayed in the field, introducing scrum practices to numerous companies, including such small-time outfits as Oracle, Microsoft and Adobe.

Of course, neither Sutherland nor Schwaber—nor anyone else for that matter—can lay claim to owning scrum, and many others have contributed to its growth over the years. The Scrum Alliance's successful certification program has led most scrum practitioners to consider Ken Schwaber's early version of scrum to be the *de facto* canon, but even Schwaber himself has at times taken issue with some of the original concepts as described in his early work. In the good old days, for example, Schwaber declared that scrum consisted of three roles, three ceremonies and three artifacts. This means that to purists, the ceremonies consist solely of the sprint planning meeting, the daily scrum, and the sprint review. But most practitioners today—including Schwaber—would agree that the sprint retrospective should be included among the ceremonies as well. Still others would argue for the inclusion of what some call backlog grooming, or story time, while a few hard core purists would tsk-tsk at you for being so loosey-goosey with your definitions. Our response to that is: it's a free country.

People will still try to tell you what is and isn't scrum, but don't you listen to them!

6

Scrum Roles

Love is the force that ignites the
spirit and binds teams together.

~ Phil Jackson

Talent wins games, but teamwork and
intelligence wins championships.

~ Michael Jordan

SCRUM TEAMS INCLUDE INDIVIDUALS WHO HAIL from many traditional domains, and may come in with titles such as: architect, business analyst, designer, software developer, tester, documentation specialist, product manager, project manager, chief bottle washer, and so on.

A scrum team will likely need all of these skill sets, but scrum recognizes only three distinct roles: product owner, scrum master, and team member.

THE PRODUCT OWNER ROLE

A development team represents a significant investment on the part of the business. There are salaries to pay, offices to rent, computers and software to buy and maintain and on and on. The business invests this money in the team because it expects a good return, better than it could get by putting the money in the bank. The product owner is responsible for maximizing the return the business gets on it's investment. A product owner does this by directing the team toward the most valuable work, and away from less valuable work. That is, the product owner controls the priority order of items in the team's backlog.

In scrum, no-one but the product owner is authorized to ask the team to do work or to change the priority of backlog items. This necessarily means that the product owner will work closely with the stakeholders to determine what needs to be built, and when, in order to deliver the maximum business value.

It is likely that some stakeholders will fall back on old habits, and go directly to team members in an attempt to get their stuff done quickly. Team members can learn to redirect these requests with artfully diplomatic ripostes like: "This sounds important, you should bring it to our product owner!"

The product owner makes sure that the needs of the customers and end-users are understood by the team. The product owner may do this directly by creating, refining, and communicating requirements. They may also do this indirectly, though collaboration with user experience professionals, business analysts, and subject matter experts. Either way, it's the product owner's responsibility to make sure that requirements are available and understood by the team. This means the product owner must be available to the team, in order to field the many questions that will come up during the sprint.

The product owner is the keeper of the product vision. This vision encompasses who the product is being built for, why they need it, and how they will use it. It informs all of the many decisions that must be made in order to make the product a reality.

If this sounds like a big job, well, it is! In our experience, this is usually the most demanding role on a scrum team. There is a natural tension between the product owner and the rest of the team; the product owner always wants more, and the team must defend its sustainable pace. This tension is healthy, so long as neither side dominates.

Due to this tension, as well as the sheer size of the job, it is important that the product owner be a non-coding team member. That is, it usually doesn't work to have a working developer also serve as the team's product owner. This goes double for combining the roles of product owner and scrum master. We have seen a few examples of teams trying to have one person serve as both scrum master and product owner. In all the cases we have seen, this has failed.

Agile coach Simon Baker elegantly describes the role of the product owner: "You must recognize that through your actions—writing user stories and acceptance tests, prioritizing user stories by business value, deciding which user stories are developed next, providing rapid feedback, etc—you are effectively steering the project and are ultimately responsible for the business value that is delivered. As the driving force behind the project your presence must be visible, vocal and objective."

The Product Owner Role in a Nutshell

holds the vision for the product
represents the business
represents the customers
owns the product backlog
prioritizes stories
creates acceptance criteria for stories
is available to answer team members' questions

The Scrum Master Role

The scrum master acts as a coach, guiding the team to ever-higher levels of cohesiveness, self-organization, and performance. While a team's deliverable is the product, a scrum master's deliverable is the self-organizing team.

The scrum master is the team's good shepherd, its champion, guardian, facilitator, and scrum expert. The scrum master is not—we repeat, not—the team's boss. This is a peer position on the team, set apart by responsibilities, not rank. Certainly the scrum master brings a type of leadership to the team, but this is strictly leadership through influence, not authority or "position power."

Why are we fussing so over the non-hierarchical nature of the scrum master role? Because the presence of rank and authority would actually hinder the scrum master in gaining the kind of intimacy and access needed to be a trusted advisor, arbitrator, and team advocate.

The scrum master is available to "hold space" for the team, to use the woo-woo term. They do this by keeping an eye on processes and progress, advising the team through hiccups and serving as a sounding board when one is needed.

The scrum master is the team's scrum expert and helps the team get the most value possible out of scrum, performing many functions, including: facilitating scrum meetings; helping the team understand and use the artifacts of scrum; guiding the other team members, including the product owner, toward a better understanding of their roles on the scrum team. Scrum masters should avoid becoming the "scrum police" scolding the team for "doing scrum wrong"; nobody wants that!

As a team becomes high-performing and more self-managing, they may no longer need the scrum master to run the scrum meetings. A good scrum master will step back and encourage this. In fact, a good scrum master is constantly adapting their style to fit the needs of their team. A new scrum team is likely to need the scrum master to do more teaching and directing. As the team develops skills and understanding of scrum, the scrum master adjusts their approach, becoming a sounding board and on-demand advisor, but pushing decisions back to the team members to make.

Another key function of the scrum master is to remove impediments for the team. Impediments are things that slow the team down, and they can come in all shapes and sizes. They often surface during the daily scrum: perhaps a team member is blocked waiting for the database administrators to approve a change; the scrum master might escalate the issue to get it resolved. Perhaps a team member's hard drive has crashed; the scrum master might help get a new PC, or even install a replacement hard drive. If the team is wasting time filling out pointless TPS reports, the scrum master will work with management to remove this burden from the team. Sometimes, the impediment is internal to the team:

perhaps their lack of testing is slowing them down. The scrum master works to help the team see the problem, and encourages the team to find a solution.

It is possible for a scrum master to have contributor duties as well. This situation is sometimes called the working scrum master, or the contributor-scrum master. While we have seen this work just fine, there are some serious draw-backs. When the going gets rough, and the deadlines are looming, a contributor-scrum master is likely to focus on getting his or her own deliverables, such as code, out the door. Yet this is the time when the team needs their scrum master most! In order to be successful, a contributor-scrum master must put the needs and success of the team above the desire to directly contribute. This is a lot to ask of someone who enjoys their technical work.

Some organizations feel that they are being more efficient"by using contributor-scrum masters. We feel this is a case of being penny-wise and pound-foolish, as an effective scrum master increases the performance of the whole team. We see very few teams that are performing so highly that they can't benefit from a full-time scrum master's coaching and impediment-busting.

THE SCRUM MASTER ROLE IN A NUTSHELL

scrum expert and advisor
coach
impediment bulldozer
facilitator

THE TEAM MEMBER ROLE

Scrum teams are highly collaborative; they are also self-organizing. Team members have total authority over how the work gets done. The team alone decides which tools and techniques to use, and which team members will work on which tasks. The theory is that the people who do the work are the highest authorities on how best to do it.

Team members, those doing the implementation work, are also in charge of estimating how much work each feature will take to implement. The product owner may choose the order of stories, but only the developers can say how large an undertaking each feature or task might be.

So how many team members should a scrum team have? The common rule of thumb is seven, plus or minus two. That is, from five to nine. Fewer team members and the team may not have enough variety of skills to do all of the work needed to complete user stories. More team members and the communication overhead starts to get excessive. Keep in mind, this is just a guideline; we have seen successful teams that had fewer or more team members.

In a traditional, siloed organization people are prone to saying things like, "Not my department, pal!" or "No way, bud! That's below my pay grade." To say something like that on a Scrum team would be a) terribly un-cool and b) nonsensical, because on a scrum team, everybody's "job" is the same: to help the team deliver the stories they committed to for the sprint.

A student in one of our Certified ScrumMaster workshops once said: "Being a scrum team member isn't about getting *your* job done, it's about getting *the* job done." We couldn't agree more.

Each team member brings unique skills and experience to the team. These strengths will help the team to do its job of delivering user stories. However, these areas of expertise should not be treated as limitations, restricting the type of contributions that a team member will make.

Back to our scrum team for an example: Justus is an expert Visual Basic (VB) programmer. Last sprint, his team took on several stories that required VB coding. Justus spent most of that sprint writing VB. This sprint, there aren't any stories that require VB code to be written. This sprint's stories require an unusual amount of testing; perhaps Justus will help with the testing work. While it isn't his primary area of expertise, it is what his team needs this sprint.

"Wait a minute!" our cost accountant says, "Aren't we under-utilizing Justus? Shouldn't he be doing the 'higher value' coding work?" Let's think about this. If Justus finds some story to work on that does need VB coding, how does this impact our team? Justus would be working on a lower priority story. We already have said that none of the stories in this sprint, those identified by the product owner as highest priority, need any VB coding. Therefore, whatever VB story Justus finds is lower priority—of less value—than the stories scheduled for this sprint. Since Justus won't be helping with the testing, which is the bottleneck this sprint, that work will go slower. What's worse, Justus' new VB code will also need testing; this will add even more testing work for the already over-burdened team. The net result is that whole team is slowed down, and produces less value, so that Justus can work more "efficiently." This is a case of a local optimization that is actually a global de-optimization.

So the team member role isn't about equality, or sameness, or an expression of any other vaguely communistic sentiment;

it is about maximizing the team's productivity. Scrum doesn't seek to make everyone on the team interchangeable, just willing to work outside of their comfort zone when that's what the team needs.

If you come to the team as a rock star Java developer, do not despair, you will have plenty of opportunities to perform amazing feats of strength and finesse, but you will also have the opportunity to share your knowledge with the team, and to learn new skills. The main reason developers take such a tremendous shine to scrum—and they do—is that it lets them see results; for make no mistake, nothing—not even love or money—satisfies a coder as much as seeing their work product up and running.

"The Scrum Team" vs "The Team"

Early writings on scrum make a distinction between "the Scrum Team" and "the Team." Ken Schwaber's *Scrum Guide*, for example, specifically uses the term "Scrum Team" to indicate: scrum master, product owner, and team members, while "the Team" refers to everyone *except* the scrum master and product owner. Few real teams shave their terminology this closely, but it's part of scrum history, so be aware of it.

The Team Member Role in a Nutshell

> *responsible for delivering user stories*
> *does all of the development work*
> *self-organizes to deliver the user stories*
> *owns the estimation process*
> *owns the " how to do the work" decisions*
> *avoids "not my job"*

THE PARABLE OF THE PIGS & CHICKENS

Don't be too quick to take offense next time someone in your office calls you a pig or a chicken; chances are they aren't casting aspersions on your appetite or your nerve. No, they're referring to a parable scrum cofounder Ken Schwaber is particularly fond of reciting. We'll let him tell it:

> *A pig and a chicken are walking down a road.*
> *The chicken looks at the pig and says, "Hey,*
> *why don't we open a restaurant?" The pig looks*
> *back at the chicken and says, "Good idea, what*
> *do you want to call it?" The chicken thinks*
> *about it and says, "Why don't we call it 'Ham*
> *and Eggs'?" "I don't think so," says the pig, "I'd*
> *be committed, but you'd only be involved."*
>
> ~ *Ken Schwaber*

By analogy, the product owner, scrum master, and team members are pigs; all other interested parties are chickens.

7

THE SPRINT

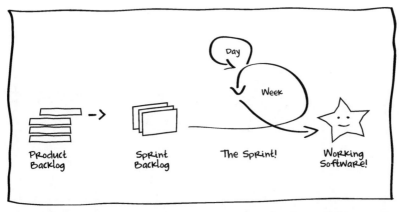

Product Backlog → Sprint Backlog → The Sprint! → Working Software!

THE SPRINT CYCLE IS THE FOUNDATIONAL rhythm of the scrum process, but the concept is not unique to scrum. If agile methodologies share one thing in common, it is an iterative approach to getting the work done. Whether you call your development period a sprint, a cycle or an iteration, you are talking about exactly the same thing: a process wherein you bite off small bits of your project and finish them before returning to bite off a few more. At the end of your sprint, you will be demonstrating working software or thy name is Mud.

We'll be using a one-week sprint cycle in all of our examples in this book. Scrum does not specify your team's sprint length, but four weeks is generally considered the maximum. Two weeks appears to be the most popular sprint length, though one and three-week cycles are also common. Much of the original writing about scrum assumed a month-long sprint; at the time that seemed very short indeed!

At the 2009 Agile Open Northwest conference, coach and consultant James Shore observed that a typical team needs roughly six sprints to become proficient with agile processes—whether the sprints are a day long or four weeks long doesn't seem to matter. Our experience is similar, which is why Chris often recommends that a team start with one-week sprints, as this allows everyone to learn and adapt to scrum quickly.

MONDAY	TUESDAY	WEDNESDAY	THURSDAY	FRIDAY
	STAND-UP 15 min.	STAND-UP 15 min.	STAND-UP 15 min.	STAND-UP 15 min.
SPRINT PLANNING 2 HRS.				
				SPRINT DEMO 1/2 HR.
		STORY TIME 1 HR.		RETROSPECTIVE 1 HR.

The table above maps out the various meetings you would schedule during a one-week sprint. You don't have to call them meetings if you're allergic to the term or consider meetings to be a form of repetitive stress injury; you can call them ceremonies, as many scrum adherents do.

The meeting lengths shown are an appropriate starting point for a team doing one-week sprints. Over time, your team can experiment and find what works best for them. The following sections for each meeting contain more details about scaling the meeting lengths.

SPRINT PLANNING MEETING

Sprint planning marks the beginning of the sprint. Commonly, this meeting has two parts. The goal of the first part is for the team to commit to a set of deliverables for the sprint. During the second part of the meeting, the team identifies the tasks that must be completed in order to deliver the agreed upon user stories.

We recommend one to two hours of sprint planning per week of development; thus a two hour meeting is appropriate for a one-week sprint, while a four week sprint may be well served by four hours. (*The Scrum Guide*, by Ken Schwaber , recommends an eight-hour sprint planning meeting for a month-long sprint.)

PART ONE: "WHAT WILL WE DO?"

The goal of part one of the sprint planning meeting is to emerge with a set of "committed" stories that the whole team believes they can deliver by the end of the sprint. The product owner leads this part of the meeting. One by one, in priority order, the product owner presents the stories he would like the team to complete this sprint. The team members discuss each story with the product owner, and review the acceptance criteria to make sure they have a common understanding of what is expected. The team members confer with each other regarding dependencies, and generally discuss what will be required to implement the story. Then the team members decide if they can consider the story committed.

This process repeats for each story, until the team feels that they can't commit to any more work. Note the separation in authority: the product owner decides which stories will be considered, but the team members doing the actual work are the ones who decide how much work they can take on.

The team's velocity, the average number of story points that they complete each sprint, is a useful tool to help the team commit to an appropriate amount of work.

Many new teams tend to over-commit. In these cases, a team member might ask, "Why are we committing to 80 story points this sprint, when our historical velocity is 55?" Teams that repeatedly struggle with over-committing and under-delivering might choose to use a technique called "yesterday's weather." When using yesterday's weather, the team commits to exactly the same number of story points than they actually delivered "yesterday," i.e., in the previous sprint. This approach is naturally self-correcting.

When we work with teams that don't suffer from the over-commit syndrome, we recommend that they use velocity as a guide, but avoid letting this single number overrule the judgment of the team. Remember, the goal is a set of stories that the whole team truly believes they will complete in the sprint.

Notice that we haven't talked about creating estimates or acceptance criteria? Really good teams have those things done long before this meeting starts. If you find that your team regularly needs to break stories down into smaller stories, refine acceptance criteria, or create estimates during your sprint planning, you will want to improve your backlog grooming process. Our suggestion is to hold separate story time meetings, which are described later.

PART 2: "HOW WILL WE DO IT?"

In phase two of the meeting, the team rolls up its sleeves and begins to decompose the selected stories into tasks. Remember that stories are deliverables: things that our stakeholders, users, and customers want. In order to deliver a story, team members will have to complete tasks. Task are things like: get additional input from users; design a new screen; add new columns to the database; do black-box testing of the new feature; write help text; get the menu items translated for our target locales; run the release scripts.

The product owner should be available during this process to answer questions. The team may also need to adjust the list of stories it is committing to, as during the process of identifying tasks the team may realize that they have signed up for too many or too few stories. If this happens, the team will negotiate with the product owner to remove or add stories—but just remember that it is important that only the team initiate these kinds of mid-sprint adjustments.

While the team makes a best effort to identify all of the required tasks, it is unrealistic to think that the generated list will be complete. Once the actual work begins, new tasks will come to light. When this happens, the new tasks are simply recorded and added to the list of tasks for the sprint. A high-performing team might expect to identify 60%–70% of tasks during the sprint planning meeting.

Some teams choose to put sizes—or estimates, if you prefer that term—on their tasks. The reason to do so is to provide predictability of schedule during the sprint, specifically so that the team can alert the product owner if they are in danger of not delivering any of the committed stories. Additionally, tasks with very large estimates will alert the team that they may want to break those tasks down further; the larger the estimate, the less well-understood the task probably is. A rule of thumb is that any task that seems larger than half a day probably should be broken down into smaller tasks.

So how to estimate tasks? What units to use? We know of three common approaches, any of which can work well, although we do think some work better than others.

Task hours. This is a traditional approach used by many early scrum teams. For each task, the team would guess how many hours the task might take, and record that as the estimate for the task. The team would then track how many task hours remained over the course of the sprint. If the number left wasn't going down fast enough, the team alerted the product owner.

Task hours, as an estimating unit, sometimes led to confusion. People often expected a task that was estimated at two hours to take two hours to complete. In practice this wasn't often the case; sometimes the task took 20 minutes and sometimes it took five hours or more. Such is the nature of estimates, which is why size estimates are often more useful than time estimates.

Task points. To avoid some of the confusion that task hours can cause, some teams estimate in task points. Task points are like story points, only smaller. Just as a team can use the *Team Estimation Game*, or perhaps *Planning Poker*, described in chapter ten, to assign story points to stories (probably during their story time meeting), they can use these same techniques to assign task points to the tasks. Such teams would then track the number of task points left to be completed during the sprint.

Task count. Some teams have simplified matters even further, and merely count the number of remaining tasks. Then they track this count over the course of the sprint. While it's true that some tasks are bigger than others, many teams seem to get a useful amount of visibility and predictability this way. This approach has the added benefit of being extremely simple; it has the disadvantage of not inherently alerting the team when a task is too large.

Which approach is best? That's a decision for the team. Remember, the goal is to get enough early warning when the team is off schedule to be able to do something about it.

The list of all the committed stories, with their associated tasks, and any additional tasks (such as improvement tasks that came out of the team's retrospective) are collectively referred to as the sprint backlog. This is the list of things the team will get done and deliver by the end of the sprint.

We've talked a lot about the team committing to deliver the stories in the sprint backlog. The product owner, on behalf of the business, is also making some commitments. The product owner agrees not to ask for additional stories during the sprint, unless the team specifically asks for more. The product owner also commits to being available to answer questions about the stories, negotiate their scope, and provide product guidance until the stories are acceptable and can be considered done.

DAILY SCRUM

The daily scrum, sometimes called the stand-up meeting, is:

Daily. Most teams choose to hold this meeting at the start of their work day. You can adapt this to suit your team's preferences. For example, this might mean 11:00 AM if you're one of those California shops where all of the developers are semi-nocturnal creatures, and that's a fine thing. Some teams prefer to hold this meeting in the middle of their day, and that's fine too. Find a regular time that works for your team every day, and go with it.

Small. Only members of the development team participate, as many people as can comfortably stand in a small circle. Don't use this method for company-wide meetings unless you plan to furnish the entire staff with orthotics.

Brief. This isn't about solving giant problems, but about keeping the lines of communication open. The point of standing up is to discourage the kinds of tangents and discursions that make for meeting hell. The daily scrum should always be held to no more than 15 minutes.

Pointed. Each participant quickly shares:

> *What I accomplished since the last daily scrum.*
>
> *What I expect to accomplish by the next daily scrum.*
>
> *What obstacles are slowing me down.*

If today's "what I've accomplished" isn't as much as yesterday's "what I expect to accomplish," we have just become aware of a slip in the schedule. With daily meetings, the most the schedule can slip before we know it is... one day!

STORY TIME

This meeting isn't usually recognized as part of scrum, but it is a great way to accomplish backlog grooming, an activity that *is* a part of the scrum canon.

Some folks simply call this meeting "backlog grooming." Jeff McKenna, a member of the very first scrum team, clued us in that calling it "story time" makes it sound like a lot more fun, and keeps the focus on the user stories. In this meeting, you will be working with upcoming stories, not the stories in the current sprint.

We recommend one hour per week, every week, regardless of the length of your sprint. You will be assigning sizes (or again, estimates if you prefer that term) to stories that haven't yet been sized. You will also be breaking the larger stories you added to your sprint backlog in weeks past down into smaller stories. The goal is to have a collection of small, well-understood stories at the top of the backlog at all times.

Why interrupt the work flow, you ask? Why not leave this meeting for the end of the sprint? Three reasons: One, backlog grooming is advance work, and it needs to be done early enough in the cycle to give the product owner plenty of lead time for incorporating the estimates into their own planning and prioritization work. Two, if your sprint is longer that one-week, several one-hour meetings will be much more productive than a single multi-hour grind. Anyone who has endured a four hour estimation meeting can attest to the pain and futility of such an exercise. Three, you don't want the end of your sprint to become a marathon of meetings.

Sprint Review

At the end of the sprint, the team has a chance to show off their work at the sprint review. This meeting is also commonly called the "sprint demo." Call it a sprint review, call it a sprint demo, or call it late for dinner, it matters not to us, so long as you make sure you have some working software to show off to your stakeholders when it rolls around.

As for meeting length, we recommend one-half to one hour for every week of development. Opinions differ on this; Ken Schwaber's *Scrum Guide* recommends a four hour sprint review for a one-month sprint.

It is good practice to invite any and all stakeholders to this meeting. The team reports which stories did not get completed, and they demonstrate the ones that did get completed.

Sometimes new scrum teams fail to have anything completed for their sprint demo. If this happens to your team, resist the urge to cancel the meeting. Scrum works on transparency, and it's important to keep our stakeholders informed, even if it is uncomfortable to stand up in front of them and declare "We didn't get anything done this sprint."

More often, the sprint demo is a celebration of accomplishments (Working software in as little as one week? Now that's a reason to party if ever there was one!), and a great time to gather feedback from stakeholders.

This is also a good time for the product owner and the team members to take notes on the stakeholders' reactions to the live product. The product owner may later make decisions about the product backlog and the release in general based on stakeholder feedback gathered during the review.

The sprint review should be a learning exercise for everyone. What it shouldn't be is a planning meeting; we gather feedback, but we don't make promises at the sprint review. Better that the product owner has some time to put the newly gathered feedback into perspective before making plans or commitments.

RETROSPECTIVE

Scrum is designed to help teams continuously inspect and adapt, resulting in ever-improving performance and happiness. The retrospective, held at the end of each and every sprint, is dedicated time for the team to focus on what was learned during the sprint, and how that learning can be applied to make some improvement. We recommend one to two hours of retrospective time for each week of development. The *Scrum Guide* recommends three hours for a one-month sprint.

The retrospective allows learning and insights to be captured while experiences are fresh, and before negative patterns have a chance to harden in place. The goal is simple: to identify one or maybe two specific things to improve, and to create an action plan to implement those changes.

Some people new to scrum have experience with traditional 'post-mortems' or 'lessons learned' sessions. These are held at the end of a long project, and often generate long lists of 'pluses' and 'deltas' that are forgotten almost as soon as the meeting ends, amidst disgruntled mutterings about "barn door" and "the horse has bolted."

While generating the traditional laundry list may be cathartic in the moment, you may find yourself frustrated to see the same items show up over and over:

> *"Once again, we didn't have*
> *enough time for testing."*

"Integrating the subsystems was painful."

*"Fixing bugs kept us from working
on the new features."*

*"It took too long to get database
changes from the DBAS."*

The problem with this kind of littany of woes is that it isn't actionable. Teams feel much better when they can identify a single thing to improve, and then immediately do something about it. Teams that effectively use retrospectives feel a strong sense of empowerment as they continually improve the way they work.

"Regardless of what we discover, we understand and truly believe that everyone did the best job they could, given what they knew at the time, their skills and abilities, the resources available, and the situation at hand."

This is "The Retrospective Prime Directive." It was created by Norm Kerth, author of *Project Retrospectives: A Handbook for Team Reviews*, and he explains it this way:

"At the end of a project everyone knows so much more. Naturally we will discover decisions and actions we wish we could do over. This is wisdom to be celebrated..."

The prime directive sets a productive tone and spirit for a retrospective. Without mistakes and shortcomings, we'd never uncover new opportunities to improve. The pain and struggle that led to learning should be honored. In this way, the team can benefit and build on the lessons and the learning that took place. If we finger-point, blame, and embarrass, people will be unwilling to share, and the opportunity to improve will be lost.

A Retrospective Agenda

In *Agile Retrospectives: Making Good Teams Great*, coauthors Esther Derby and Diana Larsen provide an excellent basic agenda for a retrospective:

> *set the stage*
> *gather data*
> *generate insights*
> *decide what to do*
> *close*

Let's look briefly at each of these. We strongly recommend reading Esther and Diana's book for a more in-depth treatment.

Set the Stage

At the beginning of the retrospective, you will want to establish a shared understanding of the goal, so that people know why they are meeting in the first place. It is always a good idea to get consensus on the goal; sometimes there is an alternative goal that would be more appropriate!

This is also a good time to identify the comfort level or level of engagement of the participants. If you find that the participants don't feel safe to speak freely, or would rather not be in the retrospective, you will likely find it much more productive to deal with those issues rather than moving ahead with the retrospective as planned.

GATHER DATA

This section is all about "what": what happened during the sprint. It's a good idea to have some structure to your data-gathering, and simple exercises like creating a time line can help keep your thinking fresh and your discussion on-topic. You can use index cards or sticky notes to build a time line of the sprint on a wall, with each team member contributing as many events to the time-line as they can recall. This helps the team remember the whole sprint, not just the most recent couple of days—or only the bad stuff!

This is a good time to bring in the team's artifacts to server as memory refreshers: burn up and burn down charts, story cards, lists of bugs, data about build breakages, customer comments, or any big visible charts that the team uses.

Esther Derby and Diana Larson's book is full of other data-gathering methods, but whatever method you use, the goal is to gather enough data to help the team see what happened as completely and from as many points of view as possible.

GENERATE INSIGHTS

This section is about 'So What?' as in: So, what does it all mean? This section is also about 'why', as in, why did these things happen? It is not about "who"—remember the prime directive and be careful to avoid finger-pointing and blame. During this phase the team will do activities designed to:

> *find patterns in the data*
> *find the most important items*
> *deepen understanding*
> *find causes and effects*
> *identify solutions or improvements*

DECIDE WHAT TO DO

The team has looked at what happened and come to some understanding about how and/or why it happened. Now it's time to pick something to do differently going forward, and to create a team-improvement task to add to the coming sprint backlog.

We have found that it is generally best to pick only one area to improve. The idea is for the team to make steady forward progress, and not to get overwhelmed trying to fix everything all at once, however strong the inclination to do so may be. To reiterate: a team that is successfully addressing one new area every sprint will feel great about it. A team that is trying to fix five areas but failing to take action on four of them will feel disheartened.

Pick things that are under the team's control, and within their power to implement. It's not helpful for a team to decide to hire more testers, if they don't have the authority to do so. Much better to pick an action the team can implement, like: "Improve our testing by automating more test cases." Be specific. The outcome of this section of the retrospective should clearly identify who is going to do what, by when.

The change you decide to implement should be viewed as a trial, or experiment. Plan a time in the near future (such as the next retrospective) to examine the results and determine if the change actually had the desired impact. Not all process improvements work as expected! If the change helped, keep it; if not, ditch it.

CLOSE

The team has done some good work. They are putting in the time and energy to continuously improve. Take a moment to recognize and celebrate this. Give the team an opportunity to appreciate each other. You want the team to walk out of the retrospective energized and more bonded than they were when they walked in.

An appreciation exercise is a good way to end a retrospective. Sound a bit touchy-feely? It is, but even cynics come around to liking the process once they've been appreciated a few times.

Invite people to call out specific things that they appreciate about their teammates. The more specific the appreciation is, the better. They typically follow the format: "I appreciate <person> for <something>." Here are some examples:

> *"I appreciate Frank for staying
> late to fix the broken build."*

> *"I appreciate Kira for being patient with
> me when I was grumpy on Tuesday."*

> *"I appreciate Kai for helping me
> debug the redraw issue."*

> *"I appreciate Justus for his deep knowledge of
> Visual Basic; it really saved us this iteration."*

That's it! With the end of the retrospective comes the end of the sprint. The team is ready to move into sprint planning and the cycle starts again; *hakuna matata.*

Abnormal Sprint Termination: When Good Sprints Go Bad

In scrum, the basic deal between management and the team is that management won't change up requirements during a sprint. In general, this works out very well for all involved.

Every once in a while, something happens that invalidates everything in the sprint plan. In these rare cases, the product owner can call for an "abnormal sprint termination." Despite the name, neither Arnold Schwarzenegger nor James Cameron need get involved.

If a sprint does end early, you should still have a sprint review if there are stories that are completed and can be shipped. Partially done work, such as incomplete or untested code changes, should be backed out. It is far better to go back to a previous, known good state than to keep half-baked work in the product.

Holding a retrospective is especially important after a sprint is abnormally terminated: because abnormal sprint terminations are unusual, they are almost always packed with things to be learned.

So, when would the product owner call for an abnormal sprint termination? Usually in response to something that happened outside of the team. We know of one team that was hard at work developing functionality to match features a competitor had just released. Midway through the sprint, their company bought the competitor! Now the top priority became integrating the former competitors features, not replicating them.

Occasionally the team will discover something that might trigger an abnormal sprint termination. In these cases, the team members confer with the product owner to see if the product owner wants to terminate the sprint. The decision to terminate the sprint early is fundamentally a business decision, so the product owner gets to make the call.

INSPECT & ADAPT, BABY

So, why do we do development work in these short cycles? To learn. Experience is the best teacher, and the scrum cycle is designed to provide you with multiple opportunities to receive feedback—from customers, from the team, from the market—and learn from it. What you learn while doing the work in one cycle informs your planning for the next cycle. In scrum, we call this "inspect and adapt"; you might call it "continuous improvement"; either way, it's a beautiful thing.

The sprint has three formal inspect and adapt cycles built in, and many informal ones as well. Here are the three formal feedback cycles:

The daily scrum marks the first cycle. This cycle is for the sake of the sprint. The team inspects and adapts what they are working on every day in order to keep on track toward meeting their goal of delivering all of the stories in the sprint.

The sprint review closes the loop of the second cycle. This cycle is for the sake of the product. Stakeholders get to see the current state of the product and give feedback. The team, and especially the product owner, then inspect and adapt the backlog in order to build the most valuable product possible.

The retrospective closes the third feedback cycle. This cycle is for the sake of the team. They use the insights gained from these experiences to inspect and adapt how they work together. This continuous improvement helps the team become ever-higher performing.

8

SCRUM ARTIFACTS

THESE ARE THE TOOLS WE SCRUM practitioners use to make our process visible. Backlogs and burn charts have been part of scrum from the beginning. We've included two more: the task board, something pretty much everyone who does scrum uses, and the definition of done, which fewer teams may yet employ, but which we find incredibly useful as a process debugging tool.

THE PRODUCT BACKLOG

The product backlog is the cumulative list of desired deliverables for the product. This includes features, bug fixes, documentation changes, and anything else that might be meaningful and valuable to produce. Generically, they are all referred to as "backlog items." While backlog item is technically correct, many scrum teams prefer the term "user story," or simply "story," and we will use these terms throughout the book. The idea is that everything in the backlog is there to help the users in some way; see chapter nine for more details. For now, it is enough to know that all of the desired deliverables, by whatever name you choose to call them, go into the product backlog.

The product backlog is an ever-changing list that is tended like a growing garden throughout the development process. The backlog changes constantly, and—like a garden—it is never finished.

The items at the top of the product backlog tend to be small in size and well-defined. This is good, as these are the stories the team will be implementing soon. Further down the backlog, the stories may be larger and a bit less defined. That's okay, so long as they get polished up by the time they get to the top. As a feature moves higher up in the product backlog, getting closer to the time when it will be implemented, it receives more scrutiny by the team; estimates and acceptance criteria get more precise, and larger stories get decomposed into smaller stories.

Items at the bottom of the backlog tend to remain more notional—at the very bottom you'll find nice-to-have features that haven't been thought out yet. Part of the beauty of the backlog is that effort is never wasted writing detailed specs for features that may never see the light of day.

Stories on the backlog are ordered by priority, and we mean a strict ordering. It is not enough to have "high," "medium," and "low." There can only be one item at the top of the backlog, and one right below that, and so on. Think of the stories as lining up, single-file, waiting to be worked on.

The product owner owns the product backlog. Only the product owner can add, subtract or prioritize items in the backlog, although he or she may do so in close collaboration with business stakeholders, customers, and the team members.

As an artifact, the product backlog may exist as a wall, a spreadsheet, or anything in-between: that is up to the product owner.

THE SPRINT BACKLOG

The sprint backlog is the team's to do list for the sprint. Unlike the product backlog, it has a finite life-span: the length of the sprint. It includes: all the committed stories and their associated tasks, as well as and any additional tasks, such as team-improvement tasks added during the retrospective, that the team plans to accomplish during the current sprint.

The sprint backlog is generated during sprint planning (see chapter seven for more on this), and once the sprint planning meeting is over, the product owner may not change the list of stories in the sprint backlog. In scrum, this is the fundamental deal between the business and the development team: the business can change direction at the beginning of each sprint, but once the sprint starts the team is allowed to focus on delivering the stories they have committed to.

One way the list of committed stories can change is for the team members who are doing the work to request a change. Perhaps the team has more capacity than they first thought, or perhaps they will not be able to deliver all of the committed stories. In these cases, the product owner will work with the rest of the team to modify the list of stories in the sprint backlog.

In contrast to the list of stories, which is fixed, the list of tasks will be ever-changing over the course of the sprint. The team will discover new tasks that need to be completed in order to deliver the committed stories and add them to the sprint backlog. Sometimes the team will realize that an existing task is no longer relevant, and they will remove it from the sprint backlog.

INFORMATION RADIATORS

Walk into a scrum team's work area and you are likely to find the walls covered with hand-drawn charts, and a task board full of sticky notes indicating what is left to do, what is in-progress, and what is done. These low-tech tools are collectively known as information radiators... if you are a bit stuffy and fond of jargon, that is. If you're not, you might like to call them big visible charts. You can bandy about either term with confidence in just about any agile crowd and everyone will know what you are talking about.

The important thing is to make these big and put them where everyone can see them. Do not be seduced by software packages that promise to chart your progress, calculate your velocity, make toast and sing Pagliacci. Even if it really could perform all these miracles, software doesn't engage as many senses as simple pen and paper on the wall. So post your charts where they can be in your field of vision all day, every day, soaking deep into your reptilian brain and keeping your whole team literally "on the same page."

Okay, so you say you are a distributed team. We're not unreasonable—go ahead and use the software, but take the larger point and try to keep as much information on the wall as you can, even if this means that each team member must keep their own task board. It's what we do at Agile Learning Labs, and it works well for us.

Burn Charts

A burn down chart depicts work left to be done over time. It plots work remaining along the vertical axis and time along the horizontal axis. In general, we expect the work remaining to go down over time as the team gets things done. This appears as a downward sloping line, moving from left to right.

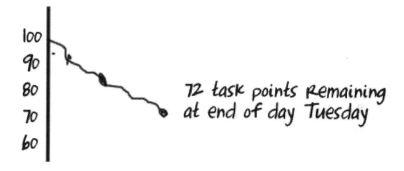

Sometimes the work remaining changes suddenly, when scope changes cause a batch of tasks to be added or removed. These events appear as vertical lines on the burn down chart: a vertical line up when we add new work, or down when we remove some work from the plan.

The reason that scope changes are vertical is because they happen essentially instantaneously: we have a meeting, make a decision, and suddenly there is more or less scope.

There are two types of burn down chart we commonly use

in scrum: the release burn down chart, and the sprint burn down chart. Some teams also use a burn up chart.

RELEASE BURN DOWN CHART

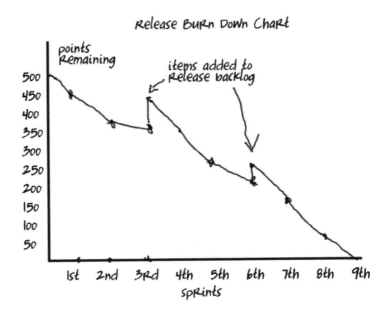

This is the tool the product owner uses to track the work remaining to be done over time. The increments of time plotted on the chart may consist of sprints, as in our example chart, but it is common for the chart to be updated daily, or even more frequently. The varying pitch of the downward trend line in our chart reflects the natural variation in points accomplished per time period.

On a release burn down chart, the jagged spikes where story points are added will be few, and will occur at the juncture between sprints.

As you move toward your release, you want to see the

trend line of work remaining go down. Keeping track of this trend line visibly and prominently is a great way of letting your stakeholders know what effect the imposition of additional requirements has on your progress toward release. It can also help a struggling team recognize problems with their productivity.

SPRINT BURN DOWN CHART

Just as the release burn down chart shows the work remaining to be done in the release, the sprint burn down chart graphs the work remaining to be done in the current sprint.

As tasks are added or completed, the team members update the chart, indicating how much work is left. The amount of work may be expressed as task hours, task points, or task count (see chapters seven and ten for more on these).

The purpose of the sprint burn down is to let the team see if they are on target to deliver everything they committed to in the sprint. If they are, great! But if they are not, this chart will help them see trouble coming as early as possible, while there is still time to make adjustments. If the team discovers that they may not be able to complete some of the stories, then they can let the product owner know right away. The product owner can then negotiate with the team as to what to do about the situation. The product owner might select a story to drop from the sprint, or may reduce the scope of one or more stories so that the team can finish them. If the team sees that they will complete all of the stories early, they can ask the product owner for another story to work on.

One surprising thing that happens in sprint burn down charts is that the trend line often moves up during the first part of the sprint, instead of down. What is happening?

While the team is doing the initial work, they are discovering new tasks that will need to be done. This is normal. As these tasks are discovered, they get sized and added to the sprint backlog. The resulting increase is reflected on the sprint burn down chart. Most teams find that their sprint burn down chart has started heading back down again about a third of the way through the sprint. While this pattern of discovering more work during the sprint may alarm some teams at first, they quickly start to recognize what a normal sprint burn down looks like: it has a hump at the beginning before things start to truly trend down.

Different teams will have different patterns. A very experienced team, working in a code base they know well, might have a very small initial hump in their chart, while a younger team working in a new area may have a much more pronounced hump.

Burn Up Chart

The team's velocity is the number of units of work (story points, for example) the team accomplishes per sprint. A burn up chart plots story points done over time, and is a visual indicator of the team's velocity. Work done is recorded along the vertical axis, and the project's time frame against the horizontal, so that you can see your progress in a line that moves up from left to right.

Task Board

A task board, like a burn chart, is an information radiator: it serves to keep everyone constantly up to date by osmosis. When your tasks are visible to everyone from across the room, you never have to look them up—all you need to do is turn your head, or get up for a stretch break and wander over.

The simplest task board consists of three columns: *to do, doing* and *done*; and the simplest way to make one is to mark off vertical columns for these on a wall using blue or green painter's tape (which you can buy at the hardware store; just make sure to get painter's tape, because it won't leave a residue no matter how long you leave it up. Use ordinary masking tape and building maintenance will be dealing with you— and they'll probably use duct tape to do it.)

After you build your sprint backlog during iteration planning, you will harvest your tasks, write them on index cards or sticky notes (the large format ones are nice), and pin or tape them in the appropriate column. Don't bother doing this neatly unless neatness is something you enjoy. It isn't important.

Now, as you perform your tasks, you have the pleasure

of moving the cards physically from *to do*, to *doing* to *done*. Trust us, everyone who uses a task board finds this gesture immensely satisfying.

A simple variation on the basic task board described above is to include a fourth column called *reported*. This is particularly useful for scrum teams who hold their daily scrum in front of the task board—something we do at Agile Learning Labs. Each person, as they report out their tasks, moves their stickies from the *done* column to the *reported* column. This keeps our cumulative accomplishments for the sprint visible, while keeping our *done* column uncluttered.

Task Board With Swim Lanes

Another common variant is to further divide the task board into horizontal swim lanes. Each user story gets its own lane, and the tasks associated with that story march across the board, left to right.

Other teams may include additional columns like: *coding, testing* and *awaiting approval.*

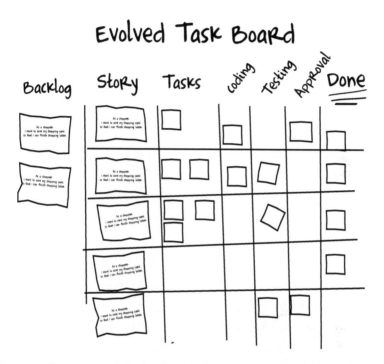

Yet another variation is the inclusion of a *backlog* column. This might include upcoming features the team could pull to work on if they finish everything in the sprint ahead of schedule.

Of course, if you are part of a distributed team, sharing a task board can be a challenge. At Agile Learning Labs, we function as a distributed team and still manage to use physical task boards quite effectively. We keep a task board in each location, and hold our daily scrum on a video call. It works surprisingly well, even though we can't always read everyone's boards. In balance, it is always better to look at a person during a meeting than to stare at a shared computer desktop.

DEFINITION OF DONE

*Doing nothing is very hard to do... you
never know when you're finished.*
~ *Leslie Nielsen*

"Hey, Fred, did ya get around to implementing the advanced search functionality?"

"I sure did, Ginger, it's all done!"

But do we really know what Fred means by "all done"? And more importantly, does Ginger?

They may be operating under entirely different assumptions. Does Fred's definition-of-done (DOD) mean he's finished coding and the feature has gone to test, but may bounce back to him? Does it mean he's demonstrated the new feature for the product owner, and met all acceptance tests for the new feature? Or something in-between?

Every team should take some time at the beginning of a project to collaborate on a shared definition of done, which should then be writ large with a broad-tipped felt pen and boldly displayed as an information radiator in the team's shared workspace.

Scrum sets great store by the concept of the team producing shippable product in every sprint. In practice, most scrum teams define a feature as done when it is potentially shippable; since it isn't always practical to actually ship features as they are completed, it makes sense to establish a set of doneness criteria that demonstrate a feature's readiness to ship, all other things being equal.

Speaking at the 2008 Chicago Scrum Gathering, scrum cofounder Ken Schwaber suggested that one's definition of done should probably include:

> *code review*
> *design review*
> *refactoring*
> *performance testing*
> *unit tests passing*
> *possibly much more*

Your DOD should be unique to your team and your project; the team needs to reach an agreement on just what is and isn't included, and that will largely depend on the nature of your product and your organization. Does documentation need to be updated? Must code be commented? Do you have customers or other stakeholders who need to sign off on a feature? Does the feature need to be included in the product's auto-installer?

It's worth noting that the definition of done is distinct from acceptance criteria. Acceptance criteria are the domain of the product owner and/or the customer, and are written to clearly define what the product must do to be deemed "acceptable." Things like regression testing and build integration do not factor into acceptance criteria.

The definition of done is owned by the development team, and addresses not the product's user-facing functionality, but the "under the hood" tasks that must be completed before the product is shippable.

If your DOD is sloppy or incomplete, then you risk accumulating a hidden pool of technical debt: tasks that lie outside of the plan and outside of your process, but which must be completed before the product can be delivered.

9

USER STORIES

*Computers make it easier to do a lot of
things, but most of the things they make
it easier to do don't need to be done.*

~ Andy Rooney

USER STORIES ARE THE BUILDING BLOCKS of the product backlog. Combined with conversations and acceptance criteria,
they are an efficient and effective way for product owners to
provide requirements to the team. Notice how these aren't
called "product manager stories" or "system architect stories"? We call them user stories to keep the focus where it
belongs—on the things real people are going to need the
software to do for them.

User stories are often written out by hand on index cards,
although some teams do opt to use software tools to record
them. Many teams use one particularly popular format for

a user story; it's not the only way to write a user story, but it is a good way. Here's the template:

As a <type of user>
I want <to do something>
So that <some value is created>

This format for expressing requirements captures a lot of information in only a few words.

The first line:

As a <type of user>

tells us who wants the functionality. Remember, we build software systems and products for people!

The second line:

I want <to do something>

tells us what the desired functionality is.

Finally, the last line:

So that <some value is created>

tells us why this user wants this functionality. Having stated who wants what, and why, here is an example user story in this format:

As a member of the Madonna Fan Club,
I want to order concert tickets by phone before they go on sale to the general public,
So that I can get great seats and feel special.

Armed with a sense of who our somewhat geriatric users are and what they value, we can create a phone ordering system that will give them a lot of value. We can have Madonna record a special greeting: "It means a lot to me that you are a member of the Madonna Fan Club. As my way of saying thank you, I'm holding a block of the best seats just for you..."

Traditional requirements often indicate the "what" while leaving out the "who" and the "why."

But maybe Madonna's fan base consists equally of old-timers and impressionable 12-year-olds who think she is retro-fabulous.

The Madonna team might push back, asking their product owner if a web-based system might not work just as well for both audiences. Perhaps the team could deliver such a system in half the time it would take to build the phone-based system.

As good as this user story template is, and we think it's pretty good, it's not the One True Way to write user stories. Any format that leads to a shared understanding, and facilitates the production of valuable software, is fine. Remember, it's not a religion; it's a tool you can use to help your team succeed.

VARIATIONS ON THE THEME

The above user story format puts the focus on the user; they are listed first. Some teams prefer to move the focus to the user's goal or the value, so they change the order around.

GOAL-FOCUSED

In order to <achieve some goal>
As a <type of user>
I want <to do something>

VALUE-FOCUSED

In oRdeR to <cReate some value>
As a <type of useR>
I want <to do something>

A User Story is a Ticket to a Conversation

User stories are not complete requirements or specifications; they are placeholders. They contain enough information to remind the team that there is something there to be done, but we intentionally don't go into a lot of elaborate detail... until it's needed.

When the time comes to elaborate on the user story, we prefer to do it in the form of a conversation between the team members involved. The goal of the conversation is to come to a common understanding of what the story is about, and exactly what needs to be done.

A live conversation is a much more efficient way to reach this goal than relying on written documentation. There is more information flowing, or if you prefer, the connection has much higher bandwidth.

Acceptance Criteria Make it Real

When you get to the point in your conversation where everyone thinks they have a common understanding of the user story, it's time to write acceptance criteria. Generate a list of pass/fail tests, written in plain English, such that if they all pass, then everyone involved in the conversation would agree that the story is implemented as intended. Acceptance criteria answer the question: "How will we know when it does what it should do?"

It is useful for every user story to have acceptance criteria written by the product owner. For stories that the team will be working on soon, this sprint or the next, these criteria should be fine-grained and thoroughly understood:

customer's email address is captured

Ideally, the team should be able to write automated tests based on the acceptance criteria, even before the functionality is implemented. For stories that are lower in the backlog, and may not be implemented soon, the acceptance criteria can be less precise; a few bullet points may suffice. Part of the work of grooming the backlog is to evolve the acceptance criteria.

Here's how to recognize an expert product owner: they have all of the acceptance criteria defined and agreed to by the team before the start of the sprint, and these don't change during the sprint. Be warned! This is not a trivial goal, and it usually takes some time before the product owner, and the rest of the team, learn what it takes to reach it.

PUTTING IT ALL TOGETHER

The user story, the conversation, and the acceptance criteria combine to form a complete requirements specification. The user story allows us to quickly, yet richly, capture ideas. In conversation we can elaborate and come to a common and actionable understanding of exactly what is needed. Finally, we capture our common understanding in acceptance criteria that are specific and testable.

10

ESTIMATING THE WORK WITH STORY SIZES

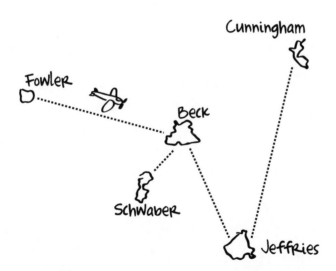

WELCOME TO THE AGILE ISLANDS! IN our workshops, we use this map to conduct an illuminating exercise in the human ability to create accurate estimates. First, we show our students this map of the Agile Archipelago and ask, "Quick! How long would it take you to get from Fowler to Beck?" Workshop participants are always stumped—it's a hard question to answer when you don't know if you'll be flying or rowing, or whether you'll be traveling in miles, leagues or nanometers.

Then, when we ask how long it will take to complete a second leg of the trip, going from Beck to Jeffries, something interesting happens.

"I can't say know how long," a bright student always pipes up, "but Beck to Jeffries looks about two-thirds the distance as Fowler to Beck—so I'm guessing it will take around two-thirds the time."

As it turns out, participants' answers are always remarkably accurate in relation to each other, even when the units of measure are unknown. That is, everyone knows intuitively that the distance between Beck and Jeffries is roughly two-thirds the distance between Fowler and Beck. So whether you're traveling by boat or by air, the trip will be two-thirds as long.

To find out "how long," the only thing to do is to make one of the journeys and see how long it actually takes. With that data in hand, our relative sizes can be used, in combination with the data from our initial trip, to provide useful predictions for the lengths of the other trips.

WHY ESTIMATE?

Why do we want estimates at all? After all, it takes time to create them. Wouldn't we get more done if we just got straight to the doing?

The real goal of creating estimates is to provide some measure of predictability of schedule. If this predictability has real business value, then it can be worth the effort required to achieve it. When there is a deadline, such as getting a product on the shelves in time for the holiday shopping season, we may have to make hard decisions about which features to focus on, and which will have to be deferred or dropped. In such a case, having some sense of the size of each proposed feature is very valuable; it enables important business decisions. This is why we create estimates: to inform business decisions, which ultimately creates more value.

RELATIVE SIZES VS TIME ESTIMATES

The traditional approach to estimation is to ask the developers doing the work how long it will take. There are two problems with this approach: one, they don't really know how long it will take. Two, they will give you an answer anyway.

It turns out that, for as good as we are at relative sizes, human beings are really bad at estimating how long things will take, and this failing is reflected in the great number of projects that run late.

While we are bad at guessing how long something will take, the good news is that we can still produce useful estimates by leveraging something we *are* good at: we are good at comparing two things and telling which one is bigger. Even better, we are pretty good at telling how many *times* bigger one thing is compared to another. Another way to state this is: while we are bad at absolute sizing, we are good at relative sizing.

The trick is to use a two-step process. First, assign relative sizes to all of the work items. The size indicates how much work there is to do. Second, do a couple of work items and measure how long they actually take. Armed with this measured amount, the relative sizes assigned to all of the other items can now be used to provide the desired predictability of schedule. This is precisely what most scrum teams do.

First they size their stories, relative to one another, a story of size "two" being twice as big as a story of size "one." The team could use the name of their smallest story as their unit. If that smallest story was "The login screen story," then all larger stories could be sized as: "two login screens," "three login screens," "eight login screens," and so on. This naming scheme works, but is a bit cumbersome. Agile developers have devised a generic unit that can be used instead of the login screen; they call it the "story point." Some developers— lazy lot that they are—have shortened this even further and just talk about "points." We will use story point and point interchangeably in the book, depending on how lazy we are feeling at the time we are writing. The important thing to remember is that teams assign relative sizes to their stories, using story points as the unit.

In summary, a story point is a relative unit of measure for the amount of work needed to complete a user story.

Second (Remember we are describing a two-part process here), the team works for the duration of a sprint and completes some stories. They can now express the rate at which they get work done in terms of story points completed per sprint. Saying "story points per sprint" got to be a bit tedious, and so the term "velocity" was coined. Now, instead of saying "our team gets 144 story points done per sprint," we simply say "our velocity is 144." It's as simple, and obscure, as that.

Your velocity is simply the average number of story points completed per sprint.

FIBONACCI NUMBERS

Let's take a break from developing software to go house-hunting in Chicago. Our first stop is the north suburban town of Skokie. We're standing on a pleasant street in front of two houses: a single-level 1950's ranch house and a two-story colonial McMansion. Can you tell which house has the greater number of stories just by looking? Of course, you say, it's obvious.

But we're city mice, not suburban mice, so we head down to tony Lake Shore Drive, where Oprah lives. Now we're looking up at a couple of high-rise towers—one is 46 stories tall, while the other is 47 stories tall. Standing on the sidewalk looking up, can you tell which has the greater number of floors? Probably not.

This story illustrates an important fact of human perception: as things get bigger, our ability to perceive fine differences in size decreases. When doing story sizing, we really can't tell the difference between a 53-point story and a 57-point story—but this won't keep engineers from arguing about it!

To put an end to such unproductive arguments on software teams, we use the numbers of the Fibonacci sequence to estimate story sizes. In the simplest terms, the Fibonacci sequence is comprised of integers in which each number is equal to the sum of the previous two: 1, 2, 3, 5, 8, 13, 21, 34, 55, etc.

The sequence was identified by Hindu scholars as early as 200 BC, but is named in the west for Leonardo Fibonacci, best known as the Italian merchant who popularized the use of Arabic numerals in the 13th century. (If you want to take a moment to thank him for the fact that you didn't have to learn to multiply LXXXVIII by XLII in the third grade, we'll wait for you.)

Leonardo first observed the sequence, which occurs frequently in nature, while studying the proliferous growth of a population of rabbits. The sequence also occurs in the curl of a seashell, the leaves of an artichoke, and the branching of a tree. You'll also find the sequence in man-made artifacts like financial analysis tools, musical compositions and trippy fractal posters from the 80's.

What matters to us, however, is that the numbers in the Fibonacci sequence, when used to represent "sizes," increase at about the same rate at which humans are able to easily perceive differences. Just as anyone can tell a one-story house from a two-story house at a glance, anyone can tell 21 story building from a 34 story building, or a 13 foot sailboat from a 21 foot sailboat, or a 34 pound dog from a 55 pound dog, or a cage with 89 rabbits from one with 144 rabbits, and so on.

Of course, by intentionally limiting ourselves to this set of numbers, we aren't saying that a given story is worth *exactly* 21 points. We are saying that it is closer to 21 than to 13, or to 34. This turns out to be accurate enough to give us useful predictability of schedule. Useful predictability of schedule, you'll recall, is what we have been after all along. It's the reason we even bother doing any of this estimation stuff.

1	2	3	5
8	13	21	34
55	89	144	?

Above is a typical set of Fibonacci cards, which are handy to have on hand at your story time meeting. You can buy them online, or make your own using index cards.

Note that the last number in our sequence is a question mark. This card stands for, "We just don't know." You wouldn't fall back on the question mark if the hand-wringing is over a question like, "Is it a 55 or an 89?" In that situation, just get over yourself and pick one (hint: choose the bigger one). You would, however, invoke the question mark if you weren't sure if the story were a two or a 144. You might find yourself in this situation when some bit of vital information is missing. In that case, you would first try to identify the missing piece, by asking yourself, "What question do we need to answer, so that we can give this item a size?"

You would then create a special kind of story called a "research spike" and mark the original, indeterminate story with a question mark.

The research spike could be something as simple as, "Ask the customer for more information," or as involved as writing a bit of code to learn more about an unfamiliar technology.

THE TEAM ESTIMATION GAME

The *Team Estimation Game* is the best technique we have found to get a team up-and-running with useful estimates. It plays like a game, but it accomplishes valuable work: assigning story point estimates to user stories.

Teams using this technique are typically able to estimate 20 to 60 stories in an hour. The game was invented by our friend and colleague, Steve Bockman. Here is how one team plays the game:

Team Estimation Game Part I: The Big Line-up

Frank, the team's scrum master, has cleared space on a long section of wall in the team room, and now the team assembles in front of it. Brad, the product owner, has brought a stack of 30 user stories from his product backlog, and the team is going to size them by playing the *Team Estimation Game.*

"Kira, why don't you go first?" Brad says, passing her the stack of story cards. Frank, who is holding a roll of blue painter's tape, peels off a small piece and hands it to her.

Kira starts the game by taking the top story from the deck, reading it aloud, and taping it to the middle of the wall. Then she hands the deck off to Kai, who goes next.

Kai picks the next story off the top of the deck and reads it to everyone. "I think this one is bigger than the one Kira just placed," Kai says, affixing his story to the right of Kira's story.

Mark goes next. The story he reads strikes him as a small one, so he places it just to the left of the others.

Now Jeff picks a story off the pile. "This one is pretty small, too." He hesitates, then moves Mark's small story further to the left to make room for his. "But not as small as the one Mark just placed."

The team continues to take turns placing stories. On Kira's third turn, she doesn't take a new story off the pile. Instead, she repositions one that is already on the wall, moving it further to the right. "Trust, me," she says, "the legacy code for this one is a mess, and we are going to have to make it all thread-safe for this story to work!"

Soon enough, all of the stories have been placed on the wall—but the team continues to take turns. Now, instead of placing new stories, they are fine-tuning the order by moving them one at a time, sometimes silently, sometimes with a few words of explanation.

"Pass," Malay says when his next turn comes, indicating that he is satisfied with the order of the stories. Justus passes during this round as well. Kira and Mark each move one more story, but pass on the next round. Eventually there is a round where they all pass. Part one of the Team Estimation Game is over!

The team now has their stories ordered left to right, smallest to largest. The story they all agree will require the least amount of work is farthest to the left, and the one that they believe will require the most amount of work is farthest to the right. What is remarkable is that the whole team has now achieved consensus agreement on the correctness of this ordering!

For those who have been paying close attention, you may have noticed that this game has the potential for an infinite loop. Mark might place a story to right, but then Kira could move it back to the left. Mark, in his next turn could move it to the right again, and so on forever. While the infinite case is theoretically possible, we have never encountered it the hundreds of times we have played the game.

TEAM ESTIMATION GAME PART II: WHAT'S YOUR NUMBER?

In preparation for round two of the *Team Estimation Game*, Frank produces a deck of Fibonacci cards. Each card in this deck has one of the Fibonacci numbers on it, from one to 144.

Mick starts off. He goes up to the wall and points to the leftmost story, vamping a bit like Vanna White on *Wheel of Fortune*. "This, ladies and gentlemen, is about the smallest story we are likely to see." He tapes the Fibonacci card labeled "1" above the story.

Justus goes next. He holds up the card labeled "2" and considers the wall of stories, searching for the point where the stories on the wall start to be about twice as much work as the story with the "1" over it. He chooses his spot, and places the "2" card above a story that lies four cards in from the left.

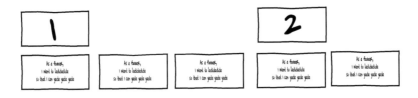

Play continues for several rounds, with each team member placing a Fibonacci card above the row of stories where they believe a size break occurs.

When her next turn comes, Kira hesitates, then points to two stories. "You know," she says. "I think we may want to reverse the order of these two. I think this one is an eight, and the other one is a 13." She uses her turn to switch the order of the two story cards and hands the deck to Mark.

Mark places the "21" card above a story. Malay is next. He shakes his head, then removes the "21" card Mark just placed. "I think this is actually a 34," he says, naming the next-highest

number in the Fibonacci sequence. He replaces the "21" card
with the "34" card.

"He's right," says Jeff.

Jeff helps Malay move the story cards just enough to create
a blank space between the last size 13 story and the first size
34 story—when the team placed the story cards in round one;
they left ample space between them to allow for this, knowing that things can shift during part two.

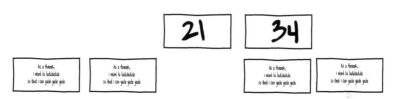

Malay tapes the "21" card above the blank space in the row
of stories, to indicate that there are no stories of that size.
When everyone has reached the point where they feel confident enough in the sizes to pass on their turn, the game is
over.

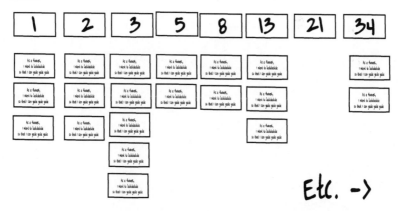

Now the team tidies up, moving the story cards to form columns under the Fibonacci cards. All the stories between the
"1" and the "2" are collected in a single column under the "1"

card; these are the one-point stories. The next column consists of all the two-point stories, and so on. The team never did put any stories under the "21, " so that column remainss empty.

THE TEAM ESTIMATION GAME: RULES

Part I: The Big Line-Up

Each player takes a turn, in which they may do any one of the following actions:

- Place a new story card on the wall.
- Move a previously placed story card. It is perfectly OK to slide cards down to make room for the repositioned card, so long as the ordering of the other cards is preserved.
- Pass their turn to the next player.

Cards are placed left to right, smallest to largest. It pays to space them widely so you can easily change the order later. Play continues until every player passes.

Part II: What's Your Number?

Each player takes a turn, in which they may do any one of the following actions:

- Place the next Fibonacci card above a story card, indicating where the next increase in story size occurs.
- Move a Fibonacci card to a different story. (The move must preserve the order of the number cards, that is, one must come before two, 13 before 21.)
- Move a story card, just as in part one.
- Pass their turn to the next player.

Play continues until every player passes, indicating that there are no more adjustments needed to the order of the stories, or the size assignments.

What we've described is the simplest form of the game. When you play it on your team, note that you don't have to start with a "1" as your smallest story size. If a player thinks there may be future stories that will be significantly smaller than the smallest story that is currently on the wall, they may opt to start with the "2" or "3" above the first story instead of the one. This leaves room for future stories to be sized smaller than the smallest story in the current set. For example, by placing a "2" over the leftmost, smallest story card, a player signals their belief that the team may encounter future stories that are half as much work to implement.

We teach this game to the teams we work with, and many of them tell us that they have never before started a project with the whole team believing that the estimates were correct. This is the way to build a plan that everyone actually believes in!

PLANNING POKER

Once you feel comfortable estimating story sizes on the fly, you are ready to move on to another nifty technique known as *Planning Poker*, an estimation game designed by James Grenning in 2002. Popularized by Mike Cohn in his 2005 book, *Agile Estimating and Planning*, *Planning Poker* is a structured game used to reach group consensus while estimating tasks. It's called poker because it does indeed involve a deck of cards—Fibonacci cards again. And since the goal of the game is to reach consensus, everybody wins.

As play begins, each team member holds a deck of Fibonacci cards. A facilitator—your scrum master, for example—reads a story aloud. Each team member chooses a card that represents their best guess as to the difficulty level of the task, and everyone reveals their cards at once. If all the estimates are the same, you're done; no need for discussion.

If there is a spread, the high and low card players get the floor to argue their cases, and after that, the game is repeated. If the new estimates are identical, voila, the story is estimated. If there are one or two who still differ, they will be asked if they can agree to the majority's estimate. If there is still widespread variation, the discussion repeats, and the game is played again. In practice, estimates quickly converge through rounds of structured discussion.

VELOCITY

Once your team has completed a sprint or two, you will have a fair idea of how many story points you can tackle during a single sprint. This rate of accomplishment is known as the team's velocity.

The product owner uses the team's velocity to help select stories for the upcoming sprint. If the team's velocity is 20 story points per sprint, for example, the product owner might choose one eight-point story, two five-point stories and a two point story. Or they might choose four five-point stories. Either way, they are able to exercise their own judgment in deciding how to prioritize the stories remaining, and which ones to bring into the next sprint planning session.

It will also become obvious, when velocity is known, if some stories need to be broken down further in order to fit into a sprint.

Velocity should never be used as a performance metric: it's not about demonstrating to management that you're working fast enough; it's about gaining predictability of schedule in order to produce more value. A new team's velocity may increase at first, but you eventually want to see a steady velocity with only minor fluctuations.

PART III:
SUPPORTING
PRACTICES

II

OK.... Now What?

SCRUM IS A LIGHTWEIGHT FRAMEWORK. IT doesn't tell you how to plan a release, or prototype a product, or write and test your code. And that's one of the things we love about scrum—the way it leaves the "how" up to the team. But if you're on a scrum team, you will need to decide how to do all of these things, so we've included this section on other agile practices that go particularly well with scrum.

You don't have to use all—or any—of the techniques we describe here in order to call yourself a scrum team. But we think that teaching you scrum without at least mentioning pair programming, test-driven development, refactoring and release planning would be like giving you the best red beans and rice recipe in the world while withholding the recipe for our grandma's corn bread. So think of Part III of this book as things that will put some extra "yum" in scrum.

12

RELEASE PLANNING

RELEASE PLANNING IS THE PROCESS OF choosing which stories (features, enhancements, bug-fixes and the like) will
be included in your product release, and when that release
should occur. Some releases are of a complete product, such
as shrink-wrapped software to be sold at retail, while other
releases are softer and will undergo frequent versioning, such
as a web service or a tool built for internal use. Usually, either
the feature set or the release date is fixed, while the other is
variable. Either way, this is a business decision.

FIXED SCOPE

If a certain feature set must be released, then the goal of
release planning is to identify the likely release date: How
soon can you deliver the must-haves? If your business plan

revolves around designing and building a better mousetrap, there is little benefit to be realized by releasing an "average" mousetrap sooner.

FIXED DATE

If the software must be released by a certain date, the goal of release planning is to figure out what can be built by that date. The need to plan the release around a date is usually due to some market window or event: perhaps you're a startup hoping to present at Demo or TechCrunch 50, or maybe you want something to generate buzz at the next Consumer Electronics Show. Or your deadline could be something serious like delivering in time for holiday shopping or tax season. Or you may know that your competition is preparing a new release, and you hope to beat them to market.

We have worked with large IT organizations that only had a few windows in a year when they could roll out new systems—miss the coming window and they would have to wait months before another window opened.

FIXED DATE AND FIXED SCOPE

When we start talking with an organization about adopting scrum, we regularly hear the objection:

"But we have fixed dates and fixed scope!"

If the date is sufficiently far into the future, and you have the ability to add enough of the right people now, then you might be able to make this work.

"No, no! We have a fixed group of people to deliver the fixed scope by the fixed date!"

This is the point where we ask how well that has been

working.

"It hasn't been working at all! That's why we are adopting Scrum!"

This is when we have to gently break the news that scrum is not a silver bullet that will magically allow a team to deliver fixed scope, by a fixed time, using fixed resources. With or without scrum, the people doing the planning have to make some difficult trade-off decisions.

THE IRON TRIANGLE

Speed, cost, and scope: these are known in project management circles as the "iron triangle." On a software project, speed refers to the time it will take to build and release the system; cost is usually driven by the number of people working on the project; and scope involves how many stories will be included. These three form a balanced equation: changing any one of the three will necessitate a corresponding change in one or both of the other two. Add some more stories to the release and you will need to add more time or more people. Need it sooner? You will need to reduce scope or add people.

Usually, adding people only works if you have sufficient time to get them up to speed and productive. In the short term, adding people usually slows things down. Because of this, and other difficulties with adding people, most release planning actually revolves around balancing scope and delivery date.

Mike Cohn, an *Agile Manifesto* signatory and co-founder of the Scrum Alliance, literally wrote the book on agile release planning (*Agile Estimating and Planning*, 2005). He recommends using a "one-handed clock" to represent the triangle:

The single clock hand can point directly to scope, if you

care only about that, or somewhere between scope and speed. Point the hand closer to scope, as in the diagram, and this indicates to the development team that the business views scope as more important than speed, but still views speed as somewhat important.

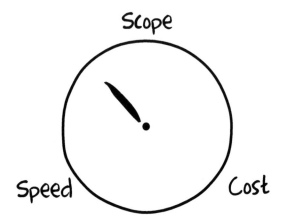

The beauty of the clock is that it can become an effective information radiator when posted in your workspace, keeping the project's values on everyone's radar.

13

User Personas

DO YOU HAVE 2.5 CHILDREN AND listen daily to the musical stylings of David Hasselhoff? We didn't think so—which is why we'd like you to take the one-size-fits-all notion of an "average user" and toss it in the dust-bin of contemporary history.

Your users, like you, are individuals. They may fit loosely into types, but their quirky behavior patterns will be the death of your software's usability, so objectify them at your peril. Instead, keep it real by developing a handful of user personas based on the behaviors of real people.

User personas are brief profiles you write up and keep at hand for easy reference. These are usually composites: fictional characters whose habits, attitudes and behaviors are based on those of real users you have studied in the wild. The use of user personas in software development was originated by Alan Cooper, who introduced the concept to the world at large in his 1998 book, *The Inmates are Running the Asylum : Why High-Tech Products Drive Us Crazy and How to Restore the Sanity.*

Here Cooper, best known for inventing Visual Basic, describes his first formal use of personas on a consulting project:

> *In 1995 I was working with the three founders of Sagent Technologies, pioneers in the field of what is now called "Business Intelligence" software. During discussions with them regarding interaction design for their product, I found myself continually engaged in a circular dialogue. I would ask them for a specific example of how someone would use their program. The answer would invariably follow this characteristic pattern: "Well, someone could create a crosstab of sales information... but it could be a chart, or if it were marketing data they could present it as a table. They could do anything!" It was almost impossible for those brilliant, logical programmers to conceive of a single use of their product when it was obviously capable of so many uses.*

Cooper insisted on meeting some of the company's prospective customers, and he found that their needs fell into three distinct groups. So he created Chuck, Cynthia and Rob, three fictional personas.

By using these personas every time he described a design problem or solution, Cooper found that his ability to communicate with his developers increased exponentially: "The results were dramatic. While there was still resistance to this unfamiliar method, the programmers could clearly see the sense in my designs because they could identify with these hypothetical archetypes."

Here are some rules of thumb for designing personas:

> *Keep your personas goal-oriented.*
> *What do they want to get done?*

> *Be specific. Give them names, hobbies,*
> *whatever it takes to make them real to you.*

> *Take notes on real users' characteristics*
> *during your requirements-gathering.*

> *Combine characteristics of real*
> *people into composite portraits.*

PRIMARY PERSONA

This is someone whose needs must be met; everyone else's needs come second. The best way to illustrate the benefits of designing for a primary persona (or two or three or seven of them, just not eighty), is to look at what happens when you don't.

When Microsoft conducted a survey of Office 2003 users to find out what new features they wanted to see implemented in Office 2007, the company received some surprising news. According to Takeshi Numoto, the product's general manager, "More than 90 percent asked for features that were already available in Office."

Numoto shared that Word 2003 had over 1,500 commands, so many that even the most dedicated power user couldn't possibly expect to find everything they were looking for. Because the company had designed Office to be all things to all people, it served none of them well. Who has time to learn the ins and outs of a productivity tool with more lines than the US Tax Code? The answer is nobody—and that's exactly who the product was designed to serve.

Had Microsoft designed their product for Betty the office manager, Drew the paralegal, and Stephen the novelist, chances are the software would have made more sense to more people from the beginning.

NEGATIVE PERSONA

This is someone who would not use the system—so don't design it for them!

This sounds simple enough, but a common trap developers fall into when designing for a generic "user" is to design the system for the user they know best—themselves. This is one of the reasons we hear so many complaints about user interfaces that only an engineer would understand.

If your product is an auto-installer destined to become bloatware on a low-end laptop (not that you'd ever build such a thing!), then Nick Burns the IT guy would make a great negative persona to keep around. Every time you found yourself itching to include a command line tool or an API, you would just need to ask yourself, "Will anyone but Nick want this?"

Conversely, if you're building an auto installer for a LAMP stack—a product only an IT guy would ever use—you might want Nick to be a primary persona. One of your negative personas might be Martha S., a professional decorator and part-time day trader who can't seem to grasp technical concepts however many times she is exposed to them. If you design your IT product with Martha's foibles in mind, inserting intrusive permissions and warnings at every step of the installation, then you might well alienate Nick, your primary user. In which case, "Are we building <some feature> for Martha?" would be a good check-in question.

EXAMPLE PERSONA

Here is an example of a persona worksheet we use in our product owner workshops:

User Persona Worksheet

Name: Wanda Bodine
Role: Sales Manager
Age: 39 (or so)

Description: Rhonda is in charge of 32 sales agents in the field. She is proud of being tech-savvy. Rhonda is hands-on with her data to a fault. she ends up working with SalesForce.com more than she interacts with her people. Rhonda is a level 68 shaman in World of Warcraft, and an accomplished amateur sushi chef.

14

STORY MAPPING

STORY MAPPING IS A WAY OF organizing user stories that provides richer context than a traditional product backlog, and can help with release planning.

Although a story map isn't necessarily a replacement for a product backlog, it is useful to compare and contrast them. The product backlog is essentially one-dimensional. User stories are organized from highest to lowest priority. A story map is two-dimensional, indicating the priority of stories, but also their relation to each other and the larger goals of the users. The map helps the team to understand how stories fit together to form a releasable product.

The process starts with identifying the users of the system and the activities they will be doing. In a 2005 article, "It's All How You Slice It," in *Better Software*, Jeff Patton gives the example of software for a retail store. The users' main activities are:

> *create purchase order for vendor*
> *receive shipment from vendor*
> *create tags for items*
> *sell items*
> *return items*
> *analyze sales*

Patton refers to these as "the backbone" of the story map. They describe, at a high level, everything that the user needs the system to help them do. These activities are recorded on cards and arranged from left to right in the order that they would naturally occur. Jeff recommends using the order that you would choose if describing the business process to someone unfamiliar with it.

Retail Story Map

Below each of these activities, arrange the associated user stories, putting the most important ones higher up than the less important ones. Now the backbone has grown ribs. Each story is associated with a user activity, and has a priority. A release plan can be visually represented by drawing a horizontal line from left to right. Stories above the line are in the release, and those below are not. In fact, several releases can be planned this way, dividing the map into horizontal swim lanes.

During the writing of this book, we used a story map to help us decide what material to include in the first version and what to save for *The Elements of Scrum 2.0*. We made the chapter headings into a backbone, and tasked out the writing, revising, research and illustration to form the ribs.

15

Paper Prototyping

MOST SOFTWARE PRODUCT MOCK-UPS ARE CREATED in HTML, PowerPoint, Adobe Fireworks or Photoshop, but consider an alternative to pixels: good old-fashioned paper. Paper prototyping removes all technological barriers and allows even Muggles who possess no magical coding abilities to participate in the design process.

Not everyone who will have input during the design process knows HTML, and even if they do, they aren't likely to jump in on the fly in the middle of a demo and redesign a page to show you exactly how they think the software should work. But everyone who has graduated from kindergarten knows what to do with a stack of paper, pencils and a glue stick. By making your prototype accessible, disposable and non-precious, you encourage participation.

Lots of people have doubtless independently "invented" this simple back-of-the-napkin approach on their own; we

wouldn't begin to know who to credit with that fit of genius, but usability engineer Carolyn Snyder has done some
rigorous thinking on the subject. Her book, *Paper Prototyping*, is the resource you will want to own and consult if you
decide to use this method, but here are some introductory
steps, based on our own experience teaching the technique
to product owners:

> *Use cheap, disposable paper. It needs
> to be easy to scrap and start over.*
>
> *Draw rough shapes and write out the
> names of buttons and features.*
>
> *You can use sticky notes to create buttons
> that can appear and disappear on a page
> depending on the actions of the user.*
>
> *Make as many pages as you need to
> create all the screens a user would
> see to complete an action.*

To demonstrate the prototype, you ideally need three people:
a user, a computer, and a facilitator.

The facilitator tells the user what they are being asked to
accomplish while using the application, like: "Make a reser-
vation for a hotel near the Boston airport."

The user taps the paper to click, and tells the computer
what to type. The person playing the role of the computer
flips or manipulates pages in response to the user's actions.
When the user wants to type, the computer writes out their
words.

The user may not ask questions of the computer or the
facilitator: the test is to see if the application functions for

them on its own.

Paper prototyping isn't part of scrum, but it is intrinsically agile, and an excellent item for a product owner's tool kit. This low-tech, high-engagement approach removes barriers to including the customer in the design and development process, and maximizes learning, as it includes a rapid feedback cycle—mere moments!

16

The Project Micro-Charter

A MICRO-CHARTER IS A BRIEF DOCUMENT that identifies key aspects of a project. A project is born as an idea; the micro-charter is a way to capture that idea efficiently. Once captured, the idea becomes easier to share, discuss, and refine, which can really help you identify and rout out scope and mission creep. It's a handy thing for the product owner to whip out when a marketing exec is pressuring her to add restaurant reviews to the traffic report website, for example.

You may have noticed that the likelihood that a business document will be read goes down as the length of the document goes up. This is why a micro-charter is micro. Even if the various aspects addressed in the micro-charter eventually get more in-depth treatments in other documents, the micro-charter remains a useful summary that can be given to anyone involved with the project to help them quickly understand the project.

A basic micro-charter includes the following elements:

code name
mission statement
vision statement
elevator pitch
business value
customers
metrics
milestones
resources
risks
trade-offs

Let's look at each of these in more detail:

CODE NAME

Give your project a name. You'll have an easier time talking about "Project X-1" than "that project idea about a flight simulator game that Chuck over in research has." Good product names take time and research to get right. We don't want to spend that time now, so we'll come up with a throw-away code name that we can use to refer to the project.

You can have a bit of fun with code names; many perfectly serious businesses do. Microsoft has used code names like Longhorn, Zamboni and Opus (Windows Vista, Microsoft Visual C++ and Word for Windows, respectively). The Apple IIc+ was fondly known as Adam Ant in-house, and the Mac II was named Little Big Mac.

If stumped, you could use the names of team members'

pets, or the names of Star Trek characters; "Project Uhura" has a pleasant ring to it. You'll even find project code name generators online that can suggest somewhat surrealistic names like "Reborn Gloomy Kangaroo" or "Tainted Weather."

MISSION STATEMENT

Your mission statement should express your project's purpose. Although your mission can be pragmatic, it can also be couched in abstract or even idealistic terms. Here, by way of example, is the mission statement for the international non-profit, Mercy Corps:

> *Mercy Corps exists to alleviate suffering,*
> *poverty and oppression by helping people build*
> *secure, productive and just communities.*

Notice the brevity. Brevity makes mission statements more powerful. Notice as well the idealistic terminology. You don't have to be out to save the world from hunger and oppression to have a mission, so don't be afraid to express yours in human terms. Here is Apple's mission statement:

> *Apple is committed to bringing the best*
> *personal computing experience to students,*
> *educators, creative professionals and consumers*
> *around the world through its innovative*
> *hardware, software and Internet offerings.*

VISION STATEMENT

Your vision statement describes the future that you are trying to create. It's a bit of science fiction, if you will, that describes a brave new world in which your project has realized its full potential. In its heyday, Microsoft's vision statement was:

> *A personal computer in every home,*
> *running Microsoft software.*

ELEVATOR PITCH

You've got a great idea for a project that your company should undertake, and you find yourself getting on the elevator with the CEO of your company. This is your chance to tell him about the project in a way that will convince him to fund it.

Your elevator pitch should be no more than a few sentences. Focus on the problem that the project will solve and the benefits that the company or customers will get. You want it to be so clear and concise that it sticks: your listener should be able to repeat the gist of it to a colleague an hour later.

Try to avoid implementation details, buzzwords, and marketing-speak like:

> *Project Rhubarb will use Adobe Air, XML,*
> *and SOA to implement a user-friendly*
> *heuristic customer-facing interface utilizing*
> *next-generation erasable floating-point*
> *access in a vertical, flexible process.*

Nobody knows what that means—or cares. A more appropriate elevator pitch should sound like something you might actually say to someone in an elevator, like:

*Project Rutabaga will save time during
the customer support process by allowing
our support staff to see and interact with
the user's computer desktop during a
support call. We believe this will increase
customer satisfaction, and reduce support
costs by ten million dollars a year.*

So, Mr. CEO, which of these projects do you think you will
fund?

BUSINESS VALUE

What this project is worth to the business—in dollars or
sense, e.g.:

*This project will reduce the amount of time
our sales people spend on paperwork by up
to 50%. It has the potential to increase their
productivity by 10%, with a net business
value of $3 million in the first year.*

CUSTOMERS AND USERS

Customers are the people who will make the buying decisions: the retailer who buys your e-commerce platform; the
videographer who uses your online backup service; the CFO
at your company, who requested the invoicing system you're
designing. Users are the people who will actually interact
with your product. Customers and users can overlap, or be
separate, and they can be internal or external.

In the following example, the customer is your own company, the users are the company's sales people, and both are internal:

> *This project develops a tool for our*
> *sales force to use in the field.*

In the next example, the customer and the user are the same, and they are both external:

> *The customer for this project is the*
> *independent financial planner. There*
> *are 250,000 of these nationwide.*

METRICS

This is where you talk about how you plan to measure the value you just stated above. What are the important kinds of data and milestones you can use to determine if the project is successful or not? Some examples: visits to the website, revenue, bugs/defects, speed/performance.

You can keep it simple; a list of bullet points will do.

Metrics are your friend—ever spend six months trapped working on a stupid project that everyone but the suit in charge knew was a waste of time? Metrics can help you avoid getting stuck building gold plated toothpicks for the executive dining room when you'd rather be building the next-generation micro-blogging platform.

MILESTONES

Milestones are important points in time. For example:

> *The product must be on the shelves by October.*

Or significant points during the project:

> *customer accepted*
> *team formed*
> *budget approved*
> *demo system ready*

RESOURCES

What resources do you have or need to complete the project as described?

> *We need three developers to work full-time on this project for six months.*
>
> *We will need server and network capacity to serve 100,000 visitors a day.*

RISKS

Risks are things that may threaten or derail your project. "Our competitor may beat us to market" is a common risk, for example. Other examples of potential risks include:

> *We lose a key developer.*
>
> *Development takes longer than expected.*
>
> *The underlying technology isn't stable enough.*

TRADE-OFFS

Trade-offs are where you realistically assess the constraints under which your team will function. We suggest using a chart based on the one below. The chart should have a row for each attribute that may need trading-off. In a typical software project these rows are: scope, delivery date, resources and quality.

Trade-offs

	FIXED	FIRM	FLEXIBLE	FLUID
SCOPE			X	
DATES		X		
RESOURCES	X			
QUALITY				X

Next, create the same number of columns as rows. Label the columns from left to right indicating increasing willingness to change. The example above labels the columns from *fixed*, the least changeable, to *fluid* the most changeable. Place x's in the table such that there is exactly one x in each row, and each column. That is, choose one attribute to be *fixed*, one to be *firm*, and so on. When the chart is filled out, you have force-ranked the attributes. In the example, the ranking from least flexible to most flexible is: resources, dates, scope, and quality.

The benefit of the chart is that it forces all constituents to explicitly acknowledge that trade-offs do exist, and to establish some guidelines for how these trade-offs will be made. Coming up with these guidelines now, before the pressure is on, will lead to better-informed decisions later.

If quality and dates are critical, it's likely you'll need the ability to adjust the project's scope, along with some serious flexibility in your budget. You may negotiate an increase in the project's scope, for example, but by using your chart during that discussion, it will be clear that such a change mandates an increase in resources, moving the ship date, or a tolerance for lower quality. You could point out that your original emphasis on dates was driven by the primary risk factor: competition. This can help your client to see that their desired increase in scope might endanger the project altogether. The trade-off chart is your best friend!

Likewise, if the budget is tight, you will have to make hard choices about what matters most to you: quality, scope or timely delivery. For more on this topic, along with a nifty way to share this information with your development teams, see chapter twelve.

17

Refactoring

ARCHITECTURES ARE LIKE BRASSIERES; THEY SUPPORT and enhance, but only if they fit well. An architecture created using big-design-up-front often feels over-built and cumbersome when the coding starts. Later on, after organic growth has taken the system in unexpected directions, that architecture can feel uncomfortable and constricting. Just as a woman needs different bras over her life, a system needs different architectures as it grows.

The *Agile Manifesto* states:

> *The best architectures, requirements, and*
> *designs emerge from self-organizing teams.*

Emergent architecture and design is the agile alternative to BDUF. The idea is that you build just what you need today, and then evolve it over time as your needs change. In this way our architecture is always appropriate, making the system easy to understand, maintain, and enhance. This requires the team to do little bits of architecture and design work all the time, leading to the kind of architecture that emerges as we go.

Refactoring is the primary technique that agile developers use to evolve the design of the systems they work on. Martin Fowler, one of the original signatories of the *Agile Manifesto*, defines refactoring this way:

> *Refactoring is a disciplined technique for restructuring an existing body of code, altering its internal structure without changing its external behavior. Its heart is a series of small behavior preserving transformations. Each transformation (called a 'refactoring') does little, but a sequence of transformations can produce a significant restructuring. Since each refactoring is small, it's less likely to go wrong. The system is also kept fully working after each small refactoring, reducing the chances that a system can get seriously broken during the restructuring.*

Here are some example refactorings:

> *In order to improve readability, change every occurrence of the variable name "x" to "CountOfActiveConnections."*

> *In order to reduce code duplication, collect common functionality from the "Triangle," "Square," and "Circle" classes into a base class called "Shape."*

> *In order to reduce code coupling, create an interface "IDataAccess" and replace*

> *all direct database calls with calls to an*
> *object implementing IDataAccess.*

These are all examples of changes that will not affect the external behavior of the system. If you have written acceptance tests to verify user-facing functionality, you shouldn't have to change any of them after making the above described refactorings.

This is how agile development proceeds, iteration by iteration—the design work is baked into the development process.

18

Test-Driven Development

THE GOAL OF TEST-DRIVEN DEVELOPMENT (TDD) is to rapidly create code that is well-designed and verifiably correct. In the simplest terms, TDD is just this: a developer writes an automated test first, then writes the production code that makes the test pass.

This cycle is often called: "red, green, refactor." The developer creates a test, and runs it. Not surprisingly it fails, and we are in the "red" state. Then the developer implements the functionality needed to satisfy the test condition. The tests are run again, and they all pass. Hooray! We are now in the "green" state.

The developer then takes a step back to inspect the architecture and design of the code to determine if any improvements can be made. If improvements are needed, the developer refactors the code, changing it's structure without changing its behavior. The tests are again run to verify that the refactoring hasn't broken anything. A developer might do a complete red, green, refactor cycle every 15 minutes.

Maintaining a blanket of protective tests allows the developers to fearlessly modify and improve the code. This enables rapid, agile development.

Yet there is another benefit to this approach. By writing the test first, the focus is put squarely on the external behavior the developer needs the code to exhibit. Once a developer really understands what the code needs to do, they are better equipped to properly design how the code should be implemented. They are using the creation of tests to drive the design. In fact, many prefer to call this test-driven *design*, or even behavior-driven development.

Quite a bit of research has demonstrated that TDD reduces defect levels without sacrificing productivity. One study of four development teams at IBM and Microsoft found that TDD decreased defects per thousand lines of code between 40% and 90%. When you consider that the bulk of development time is spent maintaining and debugging existing code, it becomes quickly apparent how TDD moves development along faster, despite the apparent "extra work" of creating the tests.

19

PAIR PROGRAMMING

PAIR PROGRAMMING IS JUST WHAT IT sounds like; two programmers writing code in tandem, at a single computer. Wait, you ask, doesn't pairing developers up on a single keyboard cut developer productivity in half? Not in the least. Pair programming produces better designed, cleaner code, more quickly. It also eliminates silos of knowledge, as at least two developers are familiar with each section of the code. The resulting code will have fewer defects, and be much easier to enhance. In almost all software projects, the amount of time spent changing code dwarfs the amount of time creating code. Reducing defects, improving maintainability, and sharing knowledge about the code all enable faster development.

There are a variety of ways to approach pairing. Our experience is that any given pair should try several approaches to see what works best for them. Here are a few of the possibilities.

DRIVER-NAVIGATOR PAIRING

One programmer is the driver, and the other is the navigator. The driver has the keyboard, and is focused on the current line of code. While the driver is working tactically, the navigator is working strategically, thinking about where the code needs to go. The navigator is considering how the new code will best fit into the architecture, looking for improvements, and considering problems that may come up and need addressing. The navigator will also catch errors and get the driver unstuck when needed. We recommend switching roles. Some pairs switch roles each time they sit down to pair. Other pairs switch much more frequently—with every function or every few minutes.

PING-PONG PAIRING

The name is apt, because this programming style very much resembles a game. What is really nifty about it is the way it incorporates TDD practices. Two developers "play" ping-pong pair programming—or P3—by passing the keyboard back and forth, challenging one another to problem solve in the following manner:

> *Mark writes a failing test, then*
> *passes the keyboard to Justus, thus*
> *throwing down the gauntlet!*
>
> *Justus writes code to pass the test, then*
> *writes another test and passes the*
> *keyboard back to Mark with a cry of, "En*
> *garde! Take that you scoundrel!"*

*Mark sets about writing code to
make Justus' new test pass.*

The two developers continue this duel until they have pro-
duced a very fine piece of code that satisfies all acceptance
criteria and passes all tests.

Developers enjoy both the game and the quality that results from the struggle to challenge each other—and the
code—with more and more stringent tests. Developer Sean
Carley described the magic of P3 by saying that "the harder
[the developers] try to push the difficult work to the other
person, the more robust the test suite and the finished code
become."

THE TDD PAIR PROGRAMMING GAME

This variation, created by Peter Provost and Brad Wilson at
Microsoft, is similar to ping-pong pairing, but has a more
flexible structure and specifically includes refactoring. During the *TDD Pair Programming Game*, the code is always in
one of two states: red or green. When there is a failing test,
the code is in the red state. When there are no failing tests,
the green state.

When the code is in the red state, the only legal move in
the game is to write code to make the failing test(s) pass.

When the code is in the green state, there are more options:

1. *Write a new failing test.*
2. *Write a new passing test.*
3. *Perform a refactoring.*

Each of the legal moves in the game can be thought of as a
state transition:

Writing code to make a failing test pass is a transition from red to green.

Writing a new failing test is a transition from green to red.

Writing a new passing test is a transition from green to green.

Refactoring is a transition from green to green.

After any of these transitions, the keyboard is passed to the other player.

FIND WHAT WORKS FOR YOU TWO

We recommend that any pair treat these patterns as starting points. Try each of them to see what feels good.

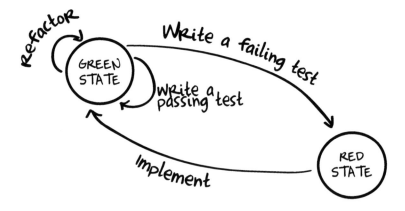

Feel free to create your own variations. Here's an example: when Chris pairs with Steve Bockman, they usually use the *TDD Pair Programming Game*. Chris, an extreme extrovert, has trouble not offering Steve "helpful advice" when Steve is working in the red state. To overcome this issue, they have added an additional rule:

> *When in the red state, only the person with*
> *the keyboard can initiate conversations.*

For Steve and Chris, this allows the person trying to solve the failing test to concentrate, and has made their pairing much more harmonious.

INDEX

Printed in Great Britain
by Amazon